# What I would Do
# If I Were You

To Jocelyn,
To laugh at something -
is the best survival
technique !

love

Mandy Nolan
2012 x

'You can judge a good woman by how many well-dressed children she has and the contentment of her husband.'
*Ladies Homemaker Monthly*

Clearly, I am not a good woman.

# What I Would Do If I Were You

## Dispatches from the frontlines of family life

Written and illustrated by
## Mandy Nolan

FINCH PUBLISHING
SYDNEY

**What I Would Do If I Were You: Dispatches from the frontlines of family life**
First published in 2011 in Australia and New Zealand by Finch Publishing Pty Limited, ABN
49 057 285 248, Suite 2207, 4 Daydream Street, Warriewood, NSW, 2102, Australia.

13 12    8 7 6 5 4

The National Library of Australia Cataloguing-in-Publication entry:

Nolan, Mandy.
What I would do if I were you : dispatches from the frontline
of family life / Mandy Nolan.
9781921462337 (pbk.)
Families--Anecdotes--Humor. Parenting--Anecdotes--Humor.
306.850207

Edited by Samantha Miles
Editorial assistance by Megan Drinan
Text designed and typeset in Minion Pro by Meg Dunworth
Internal illustrations by Mandy Nolan
Cover design by Peter Long
Cover image by Jules Ober
Printed by Griffin Press

**Finch titles** can be viewed and purchased at **www.finch.com.au**

Dedicated to my family, my greatest inspiration!
John, Zoe, Rachel, Sophia, Charlie and Ivy.

# Contents

# Happy ex-mess

Nothing fractures a family like Christmas. Every year around the country families gear up for the annual debate: who gets to host Christmas this year? In the typical nuclear family it's a jostle between in-laws and doting grandparents, both vying for this 'special' day. It usually ends in a fight about who had it last year, who's demented, who's dying or almost dead, and is generally won by the competing host who has a pool. It's like winning an Olympic bid. The victorious family shoots streamers into the sky, lights sparklers and covers themselves in fairy lights in celebration of a Christmas at home.

But compared to what I face on an annual basis, it's a relatively simple affair. In our family there are three dads, one ex-wife and numerous sets of grandparents. Christmas is a turkey shoot where every tangled strand of DNA struggles for dominance. It is the one time of year that we are reminded that we are a family which exists on the margins. We are the next generation of Brady, if Mike had already been married and Carol was a wild tart with a penchant for bad boys.

Every Christmas I am punished for being a slut. You don't have four kids to three different men and expect the fairytale. Why didn't I ever learn to commit? In *my* fairytale, a handsome prince didn't rescue the princess. She read feminist texts, had an absent father, developed a daddy issue and so tried to rescue the prince instead. Twice. The third time she settled on meeting a pre-rescued prince at the school pick up and negotiated a complicated company merger. Although I'm sure John – a single dad to a part-time daughter – would testify that meeting a separated mother with three kids was less of a merger and more of a corporate takeover. In the three years since our union he has lost 10 kilos and not had a single weekend on the couch. I just say to him, 'Listen mate, I haven't had an uninterrupted thought for over a decade.' (I'm not big on sympathy – it's genetic. Your leg would have had to be torn off with maggots feasting on your stump before my mum even considered it worthy of a sickie. As far as she was concerned if you could still hop independently you could make your way to the bus stop.)

I am the poster girl for the modern woman. Our family relationships and breakups have been negotiated without lawyer, without property settlements or restraining orders.

And boy, what an experience they were. As romantic and magical as the wedding day is, divorce isn't. If the wedding is the mouth consuming the delicious feast of love and hope, then divorce is definitely the arsehole expelling the remnants.

My day in the divorce court was like starring in bureaucratic porn. Everyone had a story, but not a good one. All of us had failed the institution of marriage and our punishment was queuing in the public toilet of love. What a group we made. I sat with the men with mullets. They chatted cheerfully and made snide comments about women taking their loot, trotting out that hoary old gag that you 'should just buy a house for someone you hate'. Across from me there were the girls so ready for a lynching they could have performed a vasectomy with their teeth. There was the girl who wouldn't stop crying, and my favourites: old men with Filipino brides. Not just one. Dozens of them, all betrayed by their egotistical optimism. Did they really think they had the goods to keep a sexy 23-year-old Asian girl in kitten heels with a fake Louis Vitton handbag, manicured nails and skintight jeans? Men really are naïve. If you want the relationship to last, get an *old* Filipino bride – one who's fat, 40, doesn't have a lap dancing career ahead of her and who won't take half your farm in two years.

And then there was me. My husband and I were the only 'joint' applicants. That meant that not only were neither of us about to kill each other, we'd both filed for divorce together. When my turn came I sat obediently in front of Mr Big Desk. He asked a few questions, read my papers and then began the few sentences which would legally undo the union that no man can tear asunder. 'In relation to the marriage from 1988.' Shit. This would happen to me.

'Excuse me,' I said. 'But you're divorcing me from a man I've never met.' The courtroom broke into laughter. Turns out the judge had mixed up my files.

Being the instigator of a family tree that looks more like lantana or an advanced game of Twister, last year I took it upon myself to devise a plan to keep everyone happy. I call it the 'People Pleaser's Christmas'. It starts on the traditional Chrissie Eve. We gather together all the kids – my three originals, Zoe (half hair iron, half mobile phone); middle biscuit Sophia (part-time real-estate agent and fairness auditor) and, dreamy eyed skateboard obsessive, the lone bearer of the X and Y chromosome, Charlie. Then there's my step-daughter, the studious, well-behaved and polite Rachel (we'll knock that out of her) and my infant, Ivy, the child of John and I, whose first words – 'Shit, shit, shit, shit' – were the only relief in the annual Mullumbimby heatwave.

Although it's Christmas Eve, we pretend it's the 25th. Wake up, do prezzies. Eat ham. Get hot. Have a fight. Eat more ham. Sophia, the child born with an internal belief system that she was meant for bigger things, scans the carnage of gifts and looks disappointed. There's a Wii Sport, but no laptop. We sit around wondering what all the excitement was about and why this much desired pinnacle of pleasure is always such a let-down. Except for the ham. The ham is excellent.

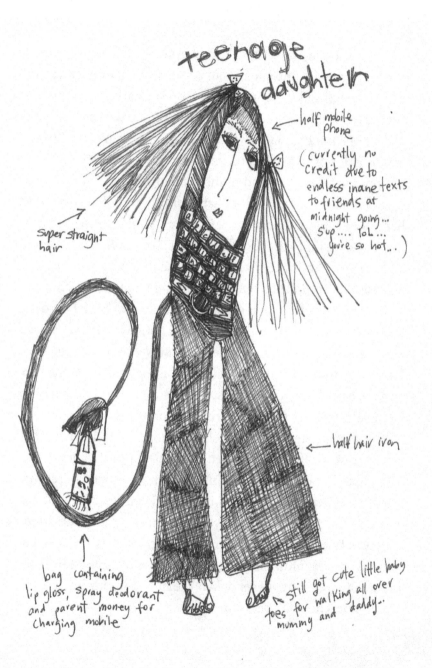

That evening, having milked the pleasure from our family cow, John and I climb aboard our seven-seater family mover and begin the journey of returns. First stop is Charlie and Sophia to their dad. (Well, technically it is to Charlie's dad, as Sophia's dad is the pot smoking, Bali-dwelling, no shoe-wearing, 'my brother was a rock star' type who turns up for the odd photo and then disappears. So ex-husband number two has taken on the father role. It's confusing explaining that Sophia lives half the time with her father who's not actually her father … but it makes sense to us.) We forge on to drop Rachel back to her mother, who is now a practising Baptist. It gives poor Rachel the value polarisation necessary to completely screw with her moral hard drive.

I hate the returns. In a separated family they're the hardest. You look at your child, this person that you love beyond words, and you know that half of their life now exists without you. There's a door to another self that a separated parent can never access. Every time I press my lips to their sweet smelling foreheads and feel them slip from my hands to wave goodbye I feel a pain so deep I can barely articulate it. As I drive away from the children that I birthed, I wonder how it came to the point that I would be delivering them to another's porch on Christmas Eve, the time of family unity. I can read the sadness etched in the corner of John's eyes and I know he feels the same. We are active loving parents trying to do our best to create a 'normal' loving family in the chaos. But it's like rebuilding on the site of a bushfire – even when the new house is built, we'll always have charcoal stains on our feet.

It's quiet in the car without the chatter of the other three. The baby is asleep. I look out the window and have a private cry. I can't really think about it too much. We head home with Ivy and Zoe who, unlike Sophia, never quite felt comfortable completely embracing the father who wasn't her father when she had a perfectly good dad who was only too ready to disappoint her.

Christmas morning we wake at 5 a.m., eat some ham and then shoot up to the Gold Coast, taking Zoe to see her hippy dad (Rhett, ex-husband number one, circa '95) and Grandma, and then fly to Sydney to be with John's family for the day. After a relaxing few hours on Wiley's Beach eating some more ham, we take a late flight full of other bloated tired peacemakers back to the Gold Coast. Drive back to Mullumbimby. Ham. Coffee. Sleep. Are we having fun yet?

Boxing Day. We wake to a fine breakfast of ham. The meat of celebration. The meat that says, 'Welcome, Baby Jesus'. We pack the car for the Woodford festival (where I have agreed to suffer the interminable heat for the sake of the two teenage daughters). But the fun is not over yet. We swing by and pick up Charlie, Sophia and Rachel from the respective exes and head north for a Boxing Day brunch with Gold Coast Grandma, Zoe and Rhett. (Please don't let there be ham. Grandma has dementia. It could be ten years old.) Rhett was supposed to prepare lunch and it does appear that there's a honey-glazed ham in the oven. But Rhett has disappeared on some bogus mission, and I suspect he's just gone looking for pot. (Let me

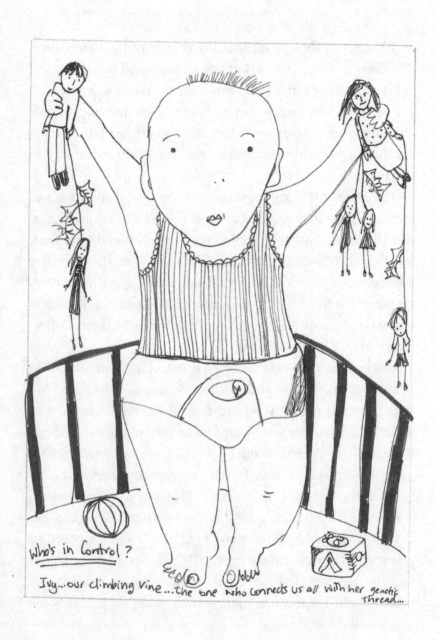

Who's in Control?

Ivy...our climbing vine...the one who connects us all with her genetic thread...

clarify, Rhett and I were never officially married but seeing as he is the father to my first two children I regard him as my official ex-husband number one).

We're hours away from creating anything that even resembles lunch so after an autopsy on the vegetable crisper I make potato salad and a dodgy coleslaw. I'm breastfeeding Ivy while I chop potatoes so John helps me prepare lunch in the kitchen of my ex's mother – I know he is truly a good man. We swim. We eat. We celebrate our strange family.

Rhett returns red-eyed, scans the lunch and remarks, 'Is this all there is? I thought there would have been more.' In the spirit of Christmas I consider headbutting him or at least performing some penetrative act with the ham bone, but am distracted when my long-suffering and patient ex-husband number two, Russ, turns up. He picks up Charlie and Sophia and takes them to their 'other' home. John and I gather up our remaining chicks, Rachel, Zoe and Ivy, and head to my mother's house on the Sunshine Coast for Boxing Day tea … with ham.

I can't believe I managed to come up with a plan where everyone gets a piece of the action. It's perfect. Shit. The dog. He's still in Mullumbimby. Christmas is going to kill me. Now pass me that ham.

# Great expectations

I never planned to have children. But then I never planned not to. I'd never fantasised about being married or wearing a white dress or living behind a picket fence and baking biscuits in the spanking silver oven of my very own home. (Ironically, now in my 40s, it's the script of my middle-aged porn). I became a feminist at 17, an existential thinker at 18 and by 19 I was a hedonistic nihilist who smoked pot, read Nietzsche and rang my mother for money. I did wear wedding dresses, but that was to lesbian debutane balls where I performed my infamous reverse strip. (This was where I came out onto the stage stark naked and got dressed. I didn't put on sexy clothes, I put on undies, track pants and thongs. It was very funny but it kind of screamed 'that woman doesn't have any material!' Literally.)

In short, I was an academic wanker with no concept of her own future and no intention of becoming financially independent. I was a very average stand-up comedian who had unprotected sex with spotty boys and when I fell pregnant, I lined up for a termination. By 26 I had had over 15 'serious' boyfriends, 30 or more one-night stands, about five attempts to be a lesbian, two threesomes, four affairs with married men, one Catholic priest and three abortions. I was perfect 'mother' material.

Then I fell pregnant again. Although I'd suffered absolutely no emotional remorse from my previous terminations, this time I asked myself a very important question: 'Do I ever intend to have children?' This was not a rational question to self. It was purely emotive. The immediate response was more like a reflex because it involved absolutely no thinking process. My mind cried, 'Yes'. The response mystified me. It completely clashed with my hardcore feminist ideologies. But here I was thinking, 'Yes, it's my destiny to be a mother.' Another philosophical triumph for biological determinism. Even the most non-maternal egg bearer like myself was seduced by the hormones of pregnancy.

You see, up until that point I'd never seen mothers as powerful self-actualised women. Or at least the kind of women I admired or wanted to be. In my prejudice, I'd seen mothers as the poor, uneducated, easily oppressed victims of a patriarchal society.

Women who'd sold their identities and sense of self down the river of role expectations and duty. These women were like the Morlocks of Well's *Time Machine*, the unseen underground dwellers. Mothers weren't clever. Mothers weren't sexy. Mothers were boring. Mothers cooked. Mothers cleaned. Mothers sacrificed. And for what? A pair of fluffy slippers once a year and a child who grows up to blame you for all their emotional inadequacies. Poor Jocasta. Even as a mythic mother she got the blame for her son's inappropriate desire to slip her the sausage. I doubt she even got so much as a new toaster for her trouble.

I decided that if I was to become a mother then I would redefine the role. I wouldn't accept the current gender definitions. As a feminist I would do things my way. What an arrogant little twat I was. I was pregnant to Rhett, a casual lover fresh out of rehab for heroin addiction. He was also the brother of a famous (now deceased) rock star. It gave him something of a mystique. He'd patted Michael Jackson's pet rat. (I can't believe I was impressed by that.) He wanted to have the baby. And so it was decided. Rhett, the long-term unemployed recovering heroin addict and Mandy the university drop-out and stand-up comedian were to have a baby.

Oh what a glorious future we offered our zygote. We were living in a converted shed in the backyard of a house that I was subletting to backpackers who got so pissed they wet the bed. I don't think for a second we ever thought about just what we could offer our baby. The decision was purely and utterly selfish: it was only about what we wanted.

Of course, our parents were delighted, although they panicked about the prospect of their grandchild being born in a manger. We thought their reactions were completely bourgeois but relented when they rented us a beautiful two-bedroom cottage for six months, complete with stained glass windows, a slate bathroom that led into a magical garden and doors that actually closed. We were free of incontinent backpackers to help pay the rent. It felt so decadent not having to check my bed for snakes every night. The week our child was born a flash flood sent a torrent of water through our shed from which we'd moved out only days before. Our beautiful newborn daughter had already saved us.

Now, as a mother in my 40s, I am shocked by my completely naïve entrée to parenthood. As I watch my sensible friends who waited for the right man and the right time grapple with painful years of IVF, I am surprised by how incredibly easy it's all been for me. It would be my only advice to women. Decide if you want to have children and then don't wait.

But then my prince was a heroin addict who stopped 'recovering' shortly after I was three months pregnant and resumed his full-blown addiction. Those glowing days of early pregnancy were marred by the incredible shame I felt for loving the afflicted. It's very embarrassing being at the all-organic natural birthing group when your partner is on the nod. I explained that he'd been DJ'ing all night at one of the local clubs and was just a bit tired. A dear friend of mine once gave me the most profound advice for dealing with living with an abusive/addicted partner: bury hope. But I loved him and believed things would come good.

Rhett promised, as junkies do, that when the baby was born he'd get clean. We had nothing. We scavenged op shops for baby clothes. We found a beaten up cot outside Vinnies which I lined with my fake Ocelot fur coat. The SIDS advisory committee would have burst a blood vessel. We smoked inside. Although I didn't use smack, I coped by smoking pot right through my pregnancy and all through the breastfeeding period. It was amazing how many velvet-wearing hippy mums vowed, 'It's safe, don't worry' and then handed me a joint before going back to feeding their unimmunised, sugar-free ADHD child.

Zoe was born after a very intense induced labour. After planning a drug-free birth like my fellow hippy sisters (ridiculous, considering I was a pot head) I begged for pethidine, hogged the gas and pushed out my 8-pound baby girl in just three hours. Nothing could have prepared me for the mind-bending pain. I panicked, but I'd survived. I didn't need a single stitch.

The euphoria when I held my daughter for the first time was unimaginable. I wept spontaneously. It was shocking to me that after nine months I'd given birth to a baby. Even now when I'm pregnant, I always find it hard to conceptualise the personhood of the creature in my womb until I see them. The whole pregnancy thing is so weird it could be a set of encyclopaedias. But a child. An actual person. It is the most ordinary miracle of all.

So I was a mother. The woman who walked into the hospital had gone. A new woman took her place. She was different somehow. Softer. Deeper. Having Zoe opened the door to this other compassionate, caring, selfless woman I'd never met before. (Thankfully she only stayed a short time.)

I remember standing in the shower and watching the water pelt down on my post-birth body. My stomach was jelly like and empty, my legs were still quivering, my vagina was engorged and bleeding. But I'd never felt more beautiful. I was amazed by my body. This was the body of Mandy the mother. Imperfect and powerful. I finally understood the foundations of the 'mother' worship.

I was stoned off my nut looking at my newborn child when I had my first panic attack. I realised that I'd spent the last six months going to birth classes, preparing for my labour which was over in three hours. What I didn't know anything about was babies. I'd never even held one. I should have been doing classes that teach you about babies. About how to bathe them or swaddle them, or how to feed them or what to do if they had a temperature. At 27, I was a complete novice. Poor Zoe was my practice child.

The fantasy of my family never matched my reality. I got Zoe home. I walked into her nursery, the one I'd placed stuffed toys and hung little mobiles in, and found Rhett and his dealer hitting up. They were sitting on the tiny baby clothes I'd laid out on the chair. I started to cry. I didn't stop for the next four years. Syringes and fluffy bunnies just don't mix.

Those were very tough years. Sure there were happy times, but it was marred by addiction and its delightful accoutrements.

I pretended to myself and the world that we were in love and things were perfect. Zoe Angel was a doll and I devoted myself to her. But we lived in poverty. Rhett's heroin addiction sucked all the cash and most of the joy. It's shameful facing Lifeline for food hand-outs and help with electricity bills on a regular basis. I made up stories about why we were broke.

Then something happened. Rhett's brother died. It was sad and shocking. It was heartbreaking. But suddenly things changed for me. Rhett decided he didn't want the squalid family life with the demanding, controlling, crying woman and the sad-eyed child. So he left. I was free.

The next week I found out I was six weeks pregnant with Sophia. Rhett wanted me to abort. But I couldn't. I was not the same callous woman I was before I had Zoe. I could not terminate the brother or sister of my precious daughter. I decided to have the baby on my own. Surely being a single parent of two children would be easier than living with an addict. I was right. It was. And at just 31 I had two daughters. I didn't have to worry about meeting Mr Right. In fact, I never wanted to meet another man again.

In retrospect, or should I say Rhett-rospect, once I got over the hurt and the anger I felt compassion for Rhett. His ongoing battle with addiction made it impossible for him to establish a normal relationship with his girls. And as for me, I shouldn't have been surprised: Rhett was an addict when I met him and an addict when he left – it was me who changed. I didn't want a dangerous, fun playmate anymore now that I was a mum.

I wanted a sensible, working, reliable dad. And in the absence of that, being a single mum seemed like a realistic plan.

I stopped smoking pot. I went to counselling. The minute I felt Sophia move inside me a mantra echoed inside my head: 'It stops here and it stops now.' I finally realised I needed to take control of my life so that I didn't destroy the lives of my children. I was consumed with a feeling of incredible urgency. I had to make it right for them. When it came to destroying my kids' lives, my dedication to the 'victim' role had made me just as guilty as Rhett. Sure, I wasn't a junkie, but by staying, I was hurting my kids. I had spent three years waiting for him to change when really, the change had to come from me.

Having a baby on your own is so different from doing it in a relationship. Even one as dysfunctional as mine had been. This time I was surrounded by my girlfriends. There were six of them at Sophia's birth. But even they can't stay forever. Suddenly you find yourself at home on your own with your new baby and your four-year-old ... and it's just so incredibly lonely. Little Sophia would smile or gurgle and I would instantly want to share it with someone, but there was no-one there. I spent hours trying to get the cat to take a photo of me and my baby.

Now I wasn't just a mother, I was a single mother. Geez, if I thought mothers weren't sexy, then single mothers were the icing on the cake. Or should I say, the cake without the icing. No-one says, 'Wow, what a gorgeous woman! And she's got two unfathered babies? Awesome, give me her number!' People looked at me with pity. It was hard. What was worse was when

family portrait I

family portrait II

they looked at me with scorn. 'Fancy having those two little babies without a dad around, tut tut.' I couldn't bear it. I closed my heart. I felt like someone who'd missed out on her turn of pass the parcel. It wasn't fair. Why me? Why was life so tough for me? I could feel the bitterness edging around my mouth. I swear it got tighter. My sleep was always broken and I had to kill my own spiders.

Then I met Russ. He was a TV director living in Sydney. We'd met before when I was with Rhett and although he later confessed to having had a crush on me for some time, I have to admit I'd never really noticed him romantically. He had moved to Byron for a few months to write a film script. I was one of the few people he knew in the area so he took to visiting me. Childless, handsome, successful: Russ was the perfect bachelor. And here he was coming around visiting me. I was like the spider who'd lured lunch into her web. I couldn't believe it. He cooked dinner, he played with the baby and he acted in the way I fantasised a man acts with a family. I fell in love. But I imagined it was hopeless – I mean who would want to hook up with a financially challenged country town single mum with two little kids and a junkie for an ex? Certainly not some hotshot director. However, six months later Russ moved in. He became a father to my daughters, who have called him 'Dad' ever since.

We were blissfully happy. It was the summer of 2000 … then it all went a little pear-shaped. Russ found out his mother was dying and was plunged into instant despair and depression.

Then I discovered I was pregnant with Charlie. We decided to move to Sydney, so Russ could be closer to his mum and his work. Charlie was born at Randwick Royal Hospital for Women in just an hour and a half in the water. He was gorgeous. And huge. He weighed 11 pounds. He was the biggest baby they'd had in the last six months. It was like giving birth to a giant fish. Everyone wanted to have a look at him. I even had canteen staff knocking on my door for a gander.

Russ's mum died seven weeks later. It was terrible for Russ. He experienced the birth of his son and the loss of his mum all in the space of two months. He was working 16-hour days on a series and had been torn between his demanding partner and his dying mother. I hated living in Sydney. Living in northern NSW, I'd always felt like a normal part of the community. But in the city, I felt like a madwoman relegated to shopping centres and indoor playgrounds. I once joined a playgroup and thought I'd made friends, but three weeks later I discovered that the women weren't mothers at all – they were nannies. Russ was grieving for his mother. I was grieving for Byron. In Byron I was a stand-up comedian, a mother and a person. But in Sydney I was just a fat, suburban cow.

Russ's work dried up. We had no income. Charlie was just six months old and Sophia was only two and a half. Zoe was at school, but I couldn't really work as Charlie was one of those babies that wouldn't let me put him down. I breastfed him for 12 months, nonstop. I don't think he slept longer than 20 minutes on his own in the first year. We started living on credit cards. It was looking dire. Poor Russ was becoming more despondent. We were living in a tiny two-bedroom cottage in the inner west, and every day I dusted the shelves which were coated with black grime that had drifted in from the Hume Highway. It settled in my hair. On my skin. In my babies lungs.

I wake up one day feeling peculiar. Like I couldn't take a deep breath. My heart was racing. I went to the doctor and then was rushed to hospital in an ambulance. I had atriol fibulation. The hippy in me thought, 'My heart can't take it, I have to leave the city.' I was cardio-verted under a general anaesthetic. For those not au fait with the medical procedure, it's like when someone has a heart attack on the telly and they bring in the paddles and scream, 'Clear!' Except that I hadn't had a heart attack. It was more a case of having to have my internal heartbeat reset because when your heart fibulates it can't maintain a regular rhythm. I awoke to massive paddle burns on my back and chest. I turn on the telly and watch planes fly into the twin towers. I have to get out.

Just a few weeks later a longstanding court case settles and I receive a lump sum payment of $25 000. It was a compensation for damage to my knee after falling through the staircase of the house I shared with Rhett. We needed a ticket out and I figured my knee could wait. With no work on the horizon for Russ, my health declining and the kids' idea of a top day out being a trip to the local servo for a carton of milk and a lollypop, moving back to the Northern Rivers seemed like the perfect solution.

So we rented a huge, rambling old homestead on 8 acres with a tennis court, a windmill, a rainforest remnant and a giant deck overlooking cows feasting on the lush green hills, all just a 20-minute drive from the sea. I had returned home. Russ and I were invigorated by the freedom of being able to lock the kids in the tennis court and crack a bottle of chardonnay.

These were the happiest days of our relationship. The children were no longer crammed in the back of the station wagon as we nudged forward in bumper-to-bumper traffic – they were chasing cows, running naked and free. Russ and I were writing scripts and I'd started performing stand-up again. We had dinner parties and dreamed about the future.

But eventually the rot set in. We'd become this incredible team of amazing devoted parents but we let our relationship slip. We loved each other but we fought. He was moody and aloof and I was emotionally demanding. He was angry; I was hurt.

It's hard to say just where it all started to erode. If our relationship was a car wreck, we weren't written off by a head-on collision, we were afflicted by hundreds of tiny unresolved resentments which were more like hail damage. Charlie slept in our bed until he was seven. Russ did all the cooking. I did none. We'd have a disagreement and Russ would go to the pub. I'd sulk. We never talked things through. We just got on with it. Unbeknown to us we were on course for complete relationship failure. So what did we do? We got married.

Our marriage introduced a brief romantic renaissance. I lost 15 kilos, bought a fabulous frock and had one of the best parties of my life. It was magical. Our wedding was so much fun. So full of love. It brought our family together. Russ was an amazing father. His Celtic heritage made him volatile but a fiercely loyal and loving family man.

But not long after, Russ and I drifted further apart. I couldn't imagine separating. Splitting the family seemed incomprehensible. But I was so lonely. Russ came home from work, cooked dinner and then went to bed at about 8.30 p.m. while I stayed up and got drunk. Alone. I went through a year or so of drink dialling until a girlfriend suggested that something was seriously wrong. So I quit drinking, started exercising and hoped that by focusing on myself and the kids things would right themselves. They did, but not in the way I expected.

Along came John. Gorgeous, daggy, clever, funny, laidback John. He was the father of Rachel, one of Zoe's school friends. I'd met him at the school's designated parent pick-up six years before. Although I think you were supposed to pick up your kids, not other kids' parents. I always thought he was very sexy, in a window-shopping gee-your-dad's-hot kind of way. I'd never considered taking him home and trying him on myself.

He was living with his girlfriend in Lismore, about 40 minutes from Byron. I was there putting up posters before a corporate gig at the uni and needed a quick change from my shorts into heels. His girlfriend had previously said whenever I was in Lismore feel free to pop in. So I did. But his girlfriend was gone. He was left standing in his house with his daughter. There was barely a stick of furniture left. His girlfriend had cleaned him out. He looked sadly optimistic and laughed as he held up an ice-cream scoop and a vegetable peeler. 'This is all she left. And they're broken!'

I think I fell in love at that moment, which was awkward when you're married and in a relationship you have no intention of leaving. When John and I met occasionally for coffee, I offered to match him up with one of my many beautiful, single 40-plus girlfriends. It would have been perfect. Only problem was, I wanted him for myself.

When you're a married woman, falling in love with another man is the ultimate family betrayal. I felt sick. I didn't need to actually have an affair, as just the thought of it was enough to bring on waves of nauseous, gut-wrenching guilt. However, I was unhappy in my relationship. Russ and I hadn't really connected for years. We had withdrawn so much from each other we were like strange planets still stuck in each other's orbit.

I still loved Russ, but our relationship had become intolerable. Over the last eight years we had moved from tender to toxic. The resentments were piled on top of cupboards, under beds, crammed in kitchen drawers. We were killing each other.

I spent the next few months in emotional turmoil. Russ and I fought continually. Everything I did pissed him off. Everything he did confirmed I needed to leave. The kids continued on oblivious. When you're breaking up people say things like, 'it will be better for the kids.' That's bullshit. The kids didn't really care that Russ and I were dying. Why should they? We were parents and our role was to parent. Kids don't give a rat's about Mummy and Daddy's sense of self. Kids just want their mummy and daddy, even if he is a stepdaddy, to stay together.

Telling the kids that we were splitting up was one of the most awful things I have ever done. They all cried. Zoe, who regularly screamed 'I hate you' at Russ, clung to him. My decision had affected their lives forever. Their childhood was now cleaved in two. Or three for Zoe. I wonder if this generation of separated kids will be supremely adjusted, or disconnected with no real sense of emotional home.

It was comparatively easy splitting up with Rhett as there was never a conversation about who would have the kids. He had an addiction to maintain and I could see that settled family life was not for him. I was always going to have the kids 100 per cent. I suffered, but the girls suffered more because they were denied the possibility of establishing a regular routine relationship with their dad.

Now it was my turn. I had to give up 50 per cent of my children. Russ was an amazing, loving, devoted father. Why would me being the mother make me a better parent? Why should I get the kids the majority of the time? For the first time in months Russ and I started working together, with our broken hearts focused on the kids. Sophia and Charlie were to live with him half the time and with me the other half. Zoe tried it but found that although she loved Russ she preferred to be with me most of the time.

John and I started seeing each other shortly after my split from Russ. My relationship with John caused Russ incredible pain. While he was suffering grief from the loss of his wife, I was experiencing the thrill of new love. I was ecstatic and

family portrait III

miserable at the same time. I knew I'd found my life partner in John, but I still loved Russ.

We have worked hard to co-parent effectively and maintain a friendship. I want our kids to still see us have a cuddle or sit together and laugh over a cup of tea. It's helped us all move on. Russ and I, although a little battle weary, are much better people for it. I now find myself trying to find great women to match Russ with. I don't understand why you wouldn't do this. As his ex-wife and mother to his children it makes sense that when a new lady comes into his life I should like her. After all, she will be living with my kids. And you can't always trust men alone to come up with suitable life partners.

John moved in some months later. This introduced his daughter Rachel to the mix. She was 12, one year younger than Zoe. She accepted her new crazy family with the most incredible grace. I was worried that not living with us full-time, she might find the new family set up bewildering. But I never sensed any resentment about the new people who now monopolised her father's life. Now I wasn't just a mother, I was a stepmother.

And then came Ivy. I was 41 at the time of delivery. It was my most well-managed birth. A three-hour water birth delivered with only breath as pain relief. I finally achieved the delivery I'd been practising 14 years before. It was the first labour where I felt myself enter the zone without fear. I felt like a cave woman, connecting to this ancient lineage of matriarchs through my primal moaning. I had nailed birth on my last attempt. If it was an Olympic event, I reckon I'd finally become a contender.

John, an ex-nurse, paddled around the birth pool giving me backrubs and crying at the appropriate times.

I named Ivy after my 93-year-old nanny. It didn't occur to me until much later how perfect her name was. Ivy is our climbing vine – she is the one genetic link that connects us all. The tiny baby entered the world and found herself related to everyone in our family. She's the only one who is. She is our common ground and we all completely adore her!

So this is our story. The story of our perfectly dysfunctional chaotic unit. Complete with ex-husbands, ex-wives, stepmothers, stepfathers and five semi-related children. It's the perfect happy ending to my fairytale.

# The parcel of least resilience

What I would do if I were you:
Practise random acts of disappointment

You can protect your kids against whooping cough, mumps and measles, but you cannot inoculate them against disappointment. Disappointment is something that children need to be exposed to and, like bacteria, I suggest the only way to build immunity is regular doses.

For example, last Christmas I only got one of my kids a present. As the tears rolled down the non-recipients' peachy cheeks I looked on lovingly and said, 'Mummy has given you the best gift of all. She's made you a nice person. Now you know what it feels like to miss out. It will fertilise your humanity.' It didn't go quite as predicted. Instead of fostering lama-like compassion, it instigated a frenzy between them. The joy of only one child

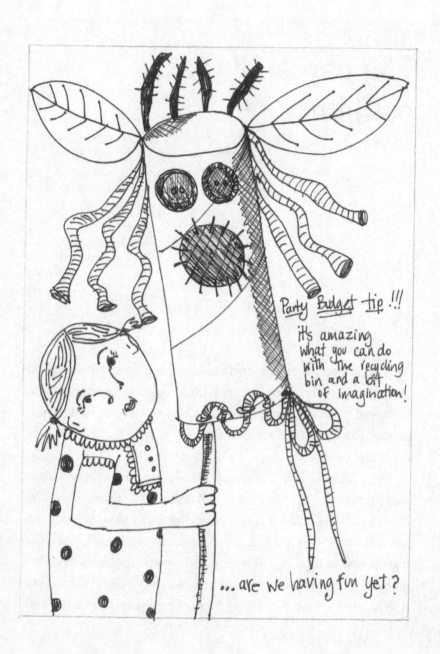

unwrapping a brand new iPod was like blood in the water. There was screaming, a bite to a fleshy thigh and tufts of hair mingled with the plush pile on my flokati. Okay. So that didn't really go to plan. (I should point out, that having children is largely an experiment. The great thing is that when you have more than one, you get a chance to get it right, eventually. Or not.)

I should also point out that, of course, I have never just given just one child a gift. It's a fantasy. When it comes to spoiling my kids, I'm as guilty as the next person. Birthday parties, or as I like to call them, platforms for embarrassing displays of social extravagance, have created an unrealistic level of expectation. Apparently my kids think they're special. Every year they expect, no, they demand, a unique purpose-designed celebration to mark their passing year. We've had a *Finding Nemo* party where everyone dressed like a fish (parents were encouraged to come as seaweed or coral to add atmosphere), about five *Harry Potter* parties where everyone came as Harry, and most recently a 'Next Top Model Party' where over 15 young girls ransacked my wardrobe and did a fashion shoot. This was an excellent party idea as I didn't have to provide food: 'Models don't eat, girls. Here, have a cigarette and a Diet Coke.' It was a little hard to explain at parent pick up and I shouldn't have told the fat kid to lose weight, but I was chanelling Heidi Klum and realistically, the girl was never going to cut it.

Parents just didn't put in that sort of effort when I was a kid. I only ever remember two birthday parties, assurance of the fact that I was not special. The first party was when I was eight. It would have been magical had I not been mauled by a passing German Shepherd and ended up at casualty. When my friends were playing pin the tail on the donkey, I was strapped to a plastic chair getting a tetanus injection.

The only other party I had was when I was 12. Mum took me, my brother and my cousin to McDonald's. We wore silly hats and sat in an empty party room clutching our balloons and ate ice-cream cake until I McBarfed all over the McPlayground. You wouldn't get away with that now. My kids would phone the Children's Helpline and cite neglect.

You can't just be a mother anymore, you need to be an event organiser. For the amount of effort you have to put in I suggest that you maximise your return. For the six weeks' party lead-in time I find that withholding the party makes a great threat. For example, I might say, 'If you don't go to bed now I'm going to cancel your party,' or 'Eat your broccoli or I'll dance naked at cake time,' or 'Give me a foot massage or I'll put kitty litter in the lolly bags.'

Little kids' parties are a breeze. When they are one or two they're happy with a cardboard box, a bit of titty and a few games of peek-a-boo. (This is also the preferred party option for most blokes.) These are the parties that you end up inviting your friends to and they get rat-arsed on chardonnay and attempt a bit of late arvo alcoholic face painting on any toddler that can be pinned down. I have photos of my youngest daughter Zoe at two, surrounded by drunks and with a head so badly painted she looks like a midget Phyllis Diller.

This is the calm before the social storm. Once the kids hit school the pressure is on. It's not enough to have a sausage wrapped in bread and sugar-fuelled free play. No. Mums need to organise games. And not just ordinary games. Games that reinforce the novel concept that everyone is a winner.

Maintaining self-esteem is not only tiresome, it's expensive. Last time I had a party I had to draw down on the asset line just to finance pass the parcel. I dropped a bundle at a bargain store, Crazy Clarkes or Manic Micks or Schizophrenic Sam, some giant stinking, toxic barn chockas full of crap. Those stores always have stuff that's so plastic the fumes are mind warping, it's no wonder the proprietor is declaring their lunacy in the shop title. A simple ten-minute game of pass the parcel can set you back a good $300. It's criminal. And, to make it worse, everyone is supposed to get a prize! That's not free market capitalism! What are we teaching our kids! A winner only exists because of the despair of others. When I was a kid only the last person to unwrap the parcel got a prize. The rest of us missed out. It reminded us that Janey had the opportunity to be successful and beautiful only because the rest of us were losers. If everyone's a winner, are you in fact a winner? In the original inequitable game of pass the parcel each layer of newspaper would bear an encryption scrawled by a ruthless parent 'to the prettiest girl' or 'for the boy with the biggest nose'. One by one the group would be whittled down into a social hierarchy of those deemed worthy or unworthy to receive the parcel. The rest of us rejects sat there consumed with rage, jealousy and

disappointment. For many, this was the place where an eating disorder first took hold. Where the cupcake became a wheat plug for grief. Where we learnt to shut our whining cakeholes with actual cake. We discovered that it often takes more than one sugary treat to hold back hurt. By the way, it's amazing how effective cake is for pain. I think they should administer Black Forest at casualty. No-one notices a missing leg with a mouthful of chocolate-coated cherries.

There's an old saying that has always annoyed me that 'there's no gain without pain'. But it's true. After every baby I've wobbled my fat arse at step classes, pulled a hammie on exercise bikes and got concussion falling off the walking machine. When it comes to bringing up kids, never forget that one truth. While it feels great to give them the latest iPod, the snazziest powerbook laptop schmacktop and a trip to frickin' Fiji to celebrate their HSC, sometimes it's best not to. Don't send them off to a five-star resort for schoolies – get them some new thongs and send them to a caravan park in Grafton. Don't give them what they want. Self-knowledge is rarely obtained in an environment of privilege. The holy man must shed his belongings and walk bare-arsed into his mountain cave. He doesn't download the latest version of iTunes and bliss out on his Italian leather beanbag at his five-star yoga retreat in Bali.

Missing out is important. Pass the parcel was not just a party game, it was a philosophical marker, a life tester. Welcome to the world of nothing. Ripping the newspaper off your parcel and being landed with a big fat zilch reminded us that life isn't fair. That the beautiful girl always gets the prize and that tubby little snot nosers like me ended up with scrunched up balls of newspaper. Ah, the defeat of promise. The sorrow of missing out! Pass the parcel prepared us for a lifetime of disappointment. So we can cope with our shitty lives, so we're not too devastated when we are not rich or get a dud job or have an ugly baby. We're not devastated for the simple reason that we were conditioned to accept that disappointment is part of life.

Lowering expectations is the ultimate antidote to depression. So start when they're young. Tell them you're going to pick them up from school. And then don't turn up. Don't cook dinner. And when they start with, 'Mummy, when I grow up I want to be famous and rich and drive a sports car and live in a mansion', hit 'em with the big guns.

'Darling, when you grow up you'll go to TAFE, get a certificate in hairdressing, live on a minimum wage, probably have two kids, one with ADD, get divorced and move back home.'

I see it as my responsibility to bring kids up with a realistic expectation about what life has in store. Wake up and smell the roses. They don't smell anymore. That's the point. Santa isn't a fantasy figure, he's a marketing ploy by Coca-Cola. As a parent it is my job to equip my kids with the skills they are going to need for the rest of their life.

You can take these grandiose philosophical meanderings and implement them like I did at the last birthday with pass the parcel. I took a more organic approach and between each layer of newspaper I placed wool or string. Sometimes a few leaves. The final prize was a toilet roll. Learn to recycle, kids. It's your future. Because life, my friends, is like pass the parcel, it's not what you get, it's what you make out of it.

# Playing house

My kids do nothing. I am their fat, white lady slave. Of course, when they see me struggling they're only too keen to help out. The other day as I breastfed the baby and attempted to vacuum broken glass from the carpet I sobbed, 'Please, someone help me!' Sophia was midway through tennis on the Wii and she slowly lifted her feet so I could vacuum underneath. The other two kids on the couch followed suit. Now that's consideration. It's fortunate for children that they don't develop empathy until much later in life as it makes watching your mother have a nervous breakdown a spectator sport, rather than something that may require physical intervention.

My children aren't completely awful. They're just lazy. If they can get out of doing something, they will. And they're not alone. From what I hear from my friends, their children are just as repulsive. In the good old days when parents could legally beat their children with kitchen appliances, the little buggers were a lot more helpful. But then they grew up emotionally repressed with low self-esteem and no self-worth and a fear of wooden spoons.

Our children are the generation who have never been smacked, sit fat and non-compliant on the couch, lording it over their grovelling parents who constantly worry that they are failing to deliver the perfect childhood. I have no idea how to illicit compliance from my children. Nothing about those ridiculous parenting books works – except using them as weapons. *Raising Boys* makes an awesome butt paddle. I not only raised a boy with it, I raised a girl as well!

Getting my kids to do the dishes takes enormous energy. In fact, if I could harness the energy and feed it back into the grid, I've calculated that it would run the average suburban home for a week. It's true. The total energy to do the dishes myself is far less than the energy it takes to get one of my piglets to do it. They're mathematicians. They know this. Therefore, continued resistance to dishwashing equals success. It is inevitable that John or I will end up scowling at the sink. I'm just not prepared to mount a battle at 9 p.m. that I know I'm going to lose.

*Note to reader*: we don't have a dishwasher. As we are in the process of building our new home, we are living in a run-down rental, a dilapidated yet charming 120-year-old relocated

the growing resentment of the parent slaves meant the children couldn't hear their movie...

farmhouse with four bedrooms and one bathroom smack bang in the middle of town. We are on the way to the local high school. Our letterbox has been blown up so many times it no longer opens properly. We are number 131, but currently we are '1 1' because the 3 was blown clean off. Our house is inhabited by two adults, three teenage girls, a nine-year-old boy and a 20-month-old toddler. We have one ugly little gremlin-like dog called Elvis, a mangey old gingernut hairball vomiting cat called Lollie and about 20 possums. The possums live in the roof with the python, who occasionally eats them. But mainly he just leaves 2-metre long empty snake skins outside my bedroom window. The possums drive the dog nuts. He yaps continually. 'Shut up, Elvis!' is the most commonly repeated phrase in our household. In fact it was the baby's first proper sentence.

Every night the possums sit on the guttering and stare at the dog with their chocolate-brown googlers. It must be like being eyeballed by a furry Marty Feldman. I thought they were gorgeous until I had to live through one of their aggressive sex romps and clean the streams of dried piss from the bathroom wall, where it had leaked through from the ceiling joins. To add to that, rats are nesting under our stove. I refuse to use Ratsak so we have to hand trap them. Right now we're pulling out about two bodies a week. Traps don't always kill them straight away. The peanut butter sandwich lures them in and then, SNAP! Another almost dead rat. The rodent drags its mangled corpse about for an hour or more, like Charlton Heston in a chariot, until it eventually expires from fatigue. It's awful, but I just can't bring myself to bash it humanely to death with a brick. Not even the cat is interested.

It's an old house, so there's no storage. Not one single built-in shelf. I bought a truckload of laminated wardrobes that looked like they came from an Alvin Purple movie, a couple of ugly pine cupboards, a makeshift linen press and coffee tables with hidey holes. Houses from 100 years ago didn't need walk-in robes or linen closets, because people didn't have anything. One pair of shorts and two shirts barely took up a drawer. But a century on we are passionate consumers. We love shit. Lots of it. Ten pairs of jeans, 40 T-shirts, 33 pairs of shoes, books and DVDs, Tupperware containers, 30 sets of sheets, 14 vases, new toys, broken toys, lost toys, special toys … under beds, on dressers. Just so much stuff. Stuff everywhere. There's even people with businesses who come around to your house and help you throw shit out to 'zen' up your life. Wow, I thought that was called a house fire.

My life is spent trying to micromanage the journey of the stuff around the house. It's a fragile balance. If the stuff doesn't go back where it belongs, it only takes a few days before a build up threatens to become an avalanche. So I spend hours every day constantly picking things up and putting them away. Conversely my children spend their life getting things out and throwing them on the floor.

Kids seem to have their own special etiquette aimed at making mess sustainable. Here are a few rules:

* When you have a shower, always grab a new towel.
* Leave wet towels on the rug.
* When dressing, try a few different outfits and leave them in crumpled piles where people walk.
* Then, walk on them. Preferably while wearing muddy shoes.
* Never get your lunchbox out of your school bag. Ever.
* Leave cups and bowls where you were eating.
* Use a new cup EVERY time.
* Leave the lid off the butter.
* Leave the milk on the bench.
* When putting rubbish into a full bin, don't empty the bin first, just shove the rubbish in so half of it hangs out.
* Never, under any circumstances, make your bed.
* When brushing teeth, make sure a large white toothpastey spit gob remains on the porcelain.
* When you do a poo, please don't flush.

I come from a generation that did what their mother told them. I wouldn't have dared to say 'no'. Not that my mother would have beat me, but I couldn't have handled the lecture, and basically, you didn't talk to adults like that, even if you thought it. You did what you were told. I'll say to the kids, 'Do the dishes.' They'll say, 'No. I did it last week. I'll do it tomorrow. Can't Charlie do it?' Then they'll make this high pitched moaning sound and their legs will become heavy and immovable. They'll collapse into a whingeing ball on the floor. They'll keep crying, 'NO'. I'll say, 'Yes you will' and

the paraplegic princess.... games about suffering
that make housework fun for your kids...

they'll say, 'No'. I'll threaten them with being grounded for a week and they'll say, 'I don't care.' And then I'll do the dishes. It's not the dishes I hate most, it's the profound sense of being a 'failure' as a parent.

My dad died when I was six. My mother was left a widow at age 26. My brother was just six months old so I had to help out. By eight I was hanging out the washing, making my bed, doing the dishes, getting breakfast, vacuuming the house and helping with the ironing. On Saturdays while Mum was at work I'd clean the bathroom and do the dusting. I hated it. But I found a way to make it bearable. I used to pretend I was a princess. A paraplegic princess. I was a beautiful girl whose parents didn't love her because she was crippled. To punish her they would make her wash her brothers piss-soaked sheets and empty the chook bucket. Returning from work my mother would often catch sight of me pulling myself up the hallway with my arms, a urine-drenched pillow slip clenched in my teeth, and simply roll her eyes.

My kids have developed this incredibly effective technique for avoiding any life skill acquisiton. It's called learned helplessness. By sucking at nearly all the tasks they are asked to attempt, there's a pretty good chance their mum will crack the shits and step in and rescue them. I've been trying to teach my 15-year-old daughter to cook just one meal. As far as she's concerned pouring boiling water on two-minute noodles is more than adequate for an independently prepared meal. But I've seen *Junior MasterChef*.

All those 'remarkable' children cooking meals that I can't even spell. They're freaks. No-one has children like that. These are the polite, well groomed children of the disgustingly middle class. It's no surprise that they're amazing. They were destined to be amazing. I think I'd have more respect for *Junior MasterChef* if they took a more Jamie Oliver approach and engaged problem children. Tantrum throwers. Biters. Kids with ADHD. Obsessive compulsive kids. Kids on crack. Just creating vegemite on toast would be a major achievement. I can just hear Matt Preston cooing, 'I love the way you've stabbed the vegemite into the toast with your flick knife ... and making a smiley face with Ritalin was pure genius!'

Zoe can't even light the stove. She's terrified of fire. One day I found a perfectly rolled joint in her top drawer. I demanded to know when she'd started smoking pot. She looked at me dumbfounded. 'The Weed Brothers (our pet name for twin emo boys who deal pot to school kids) gave it to me. I've had it for weeks. I can't even light it.' It's true. The one thing that saved my daughter from having her first toke wasn't her fear of addiction – it was her fear of fire! She can't light it! Oh, if only she had a fear of penises.

This generation of kids aren't going to be able to change a toilet roll. We do EVERYTHING for them. Sure they know their way around a digital device. They are 'Warne' fast at texting, spinning out whole paragraphs in seconds, but they can't wash their own socks. So much time is spent outsourcing our kids' leisure time to guitar lessons and soccer practice and ballet and violin and French class and tap dancing that they just don't have enough down time to learn how to be useful rather than just interesting. I'd prefer a useful child hands down.

And don't think I haven't tried all the incentive programs. I've tried sticker charts with stars where five stars equals a special outing with Mummy, I've tried pocket money, I've tried paying per household chore, I've tried withholding treats and I've tried grounding them until their room is cleaned. But they don't care. They're pigs. Disgusting filthy stinky little pigs. None of my little piggies want to go to market. They just want to sit in the lounge room and go Wii Wii Wii all the way home.

So if they won't help out, I'm planning on trying a bit of old school household management technique. All children outside. No-one's allowed inside until it gets dark. They can hang in the yard. I've bought a 2-litre pump pack of sunscreen and a cricket set. You don't get fat when you can't access the fridge. You also don't get to put your feet on the furniture, leave cereal bowls on the couch and burn up the battery on my cordless phone.

# Piggy in the middle

Guinea pigs were invented to teach children about death. If you want your kids to experience the joys and responsibilities of pet ownership then get a guinea pig and have a shovel ready. Guinea pigs are the fast food of the pet world. You've only had one for ten minutes and you already need another one.

Rodent death by natural causes is one thing. Having to euthanase a small furry beast is quite another. I've never killed anything on purpose. Sure, I've seen the desire deaden in a man's eyes after my graduation performance from my pole dancing class and I once backed over someone's cat (while it was still in their lap), but I've never consciously held a life in my hands and wrung its spirit out (except the odd husband, but that's purely on an energetic level). I am a tender-hearted woman. I can complain. But I can't kill. If I was shipwrecked on a desert island and I had to fend for myself, I'd have to nag my food to death. 'Die, die … if you loved me you'd die … you don't love me …'

It was Easter Sunday. I was hung over. The Easter bunny had stumbled through the bedrooms at 3 a.m. mildly off course after two bottles of champagne. 'Mummy, the Easter bunny left me lots of eggs … and a cigarette.'

'Clumsy bunny. Now go get Mummy's lighter off the fridge.' Toddlers are so useful.

I awoke to the bloodcurdling cry of my eldest daughter who was just eight at the time. 'The cat got Benji.'

Benji had been named after one of my son's friends at preschool. Not a good idea to name rodents after other people's children. It makes the whole thing a bit embarrassing when the namesake turns up for a play date to discover his tribute pet is two feet under in a dirt-filled shoebox. It's also a bit embarrassing and even a tad stalky trying to explain the existence of dead Benji to the mother of live Benji.

As it turned out, Benji had escaped and subsequently been mauled by the cat. He was holed up in a crevice between the trampoline and the retaining wall, his fur matted with blood, his tiny heart beating like a teenager on ecstasy. Even with my throbbing head, I could see he was in worse shape than me. *Oh God. I'm going to have to kill him.* I wrapped him in aluminium foil so as not to cause him any more duress, but couldn't help remarking how he looked a lot like a filo parcel. I put the coffee on and popped him in the freezer. If I couldn't kill him now, he'd make a tasty snack for later on.

As the caffeine took hold and the mind fuzz cleared, it suddenly occurred to me that cryogenic death was the most humane way to kill toads. Cold-blooded creatures. Not warm blooded mammals! I threw the freezer open and found the poor little fella perched up on the ice cream, icicles starting to form on his whiskers. My daughter began to sob. I tried to give her the 'cruel to be kind' speech – the main point being that one must employ some of the philosophy of Mills in ascertaining what is the greatest good. I assured her that to let Benji live would prolong his suffering. It was our job to help him find his way back home to the big hutch in the sky. That Easter morning I was Phillip Nietzsche, an unholy God whose task it was to deliver guinea pigs from evil. Amen.

'Run the bath,' I said to my five-year-old daughter Sophia, who was the pragmatic one. She was straight onto the tap, her eyes wide with voyeuristic excitement. 'Does he want bubbles, Mum?'

Zoe's grief became hysterical. Disproportionate to the size of the rodent. We'd been to the funeral of their beloved grandfather only a year or so before and I hadn't seen anyone display this degree of hair-tearing torment. I explained that I would hold Benji gently under the water and as his lungs filled with water, his small and, to this point, largely inconsequential life would pass into the ether. There was a glint in Sophia's eye.

'Should I turn the spa on, Mum?'

Images of Benji's small frame being sucked into the jets filled me with horror. God, I'd never relax again knowing that a guinea pig had met his maker in my tub. My soak time would forever be haunted by Benji's dying screams and the unexplained appearance of fur fragments.

After some time we lifted Benji's mangled body from the water, but his persistent rat heart was still beating. *Man, this little guy could have been an organ donor.* It would have been cruel to let him freeze to death so we wedged him into a cardboard toilet roll and gave him a very impressive blow dry. I couldn't help but think how much he looked like Delta Goodrem.

By now an hour had passed and all my attempts to snuff the family guinea pig had failed. Of course I'd thought about calling the vet but who wants to pay $400 on Easter Sunday for some bloke to close the door and use a brick? I should be able to do that. I remember the hands of the women in the country town where I grew up. The same fingers that could sew a hem and ice a chocolate cake could also snap a neck. It certainly made you think twice about getting pregnant to their pimple-faced sons. I thought about grabbing Benji and twisting him like a pepper grinder. (Would you like rodent on that, sir?) But I couldn't do it. Surely there were kinder and more poetic ways for our furry friend to make his way to God's big guinea pig exhibit?

Then I had it. The car! No, I was not going to let Benji drive. I'm not insured for anyone under 25 and I doubt the insurance company would fall for, 'He must have stolen the car while I was

crazed
mother
revving
vehicle

crying child

guinea pig
in exhaust

123-XX

the lessons of _Slyvia Plath_ part one: it's not as easy to gas
yourself as you think... even if you are a rodent...

sleeping' when they found him gaffer-taped to the accelerator. No, my plan was much gentler. Some may even say … a tad psychoPlathic!

For those unfamiliar with Sylvia Plath, she was a poet and a writer, renowned for writing *The Bell Jar*, famously institutionalised and finally, after a series of failed attempts, she managed to take her life by gassing herself in the oven. As a university student, like most narcissistic, self-focused 18-year-olds, I had been obsessed with the manic depressive ravings of Sylvia Plath. As a 41-year-old mother to five kids I now recognise her poetic venom as postnatal depression. Perhaps Ted could have paid her a bit more attention and seen her work as a cry for help rather than a thesis and got her some medical attention. If he had, she'd now be a fat old lady writing rhyming verse for birthday cards. 'To my darling husband from your loving wife, happy birthday, you wrecked my life.'

After ten minutes with Benji in the cooker I realised my plan would never work. I have an electric oven. I had a choice: remove him or throw in some potatoes. In a flash of genius I theorised his cylindrical little body would fit in the exhaust pipe of my car. If I gently placed him in the opening and softly revved the engine, he should fall asleep, never to awake. Like most theories, it was only a theory and after the first rev the poor little fella came flying out. Still breathing. My quest for a peaceful end for Benji was becoming sadistic. It was time to give up and let him be the auteur of his own slow agonising demise.

the suburban scream ... the unsuccessful and varied attempts at
euthanasing Benji the badly mauled guinea pig...

I tried to explain this to Zoe who, by this time, was convinced that when it came to guinea pigs, I had homicidal tendencies. She continued to cry. Benji continued to die. We emptied the uneaten chocolate from her Easter box and made a nest for her dying pet. His trust shattered, I can only imagine what the poor thing thought was coming next ... suffocation by a giant chicken, being set fire to or injected with heroin. These were all options I had considered, as it was almost noon and the hangover was fierce.

When dosing myself I had even considered giving Benji a panadol but there were only two in the pack and I ascertained that, in accordance with Mill's greatest good and for the wellbeing of the entire family, I should take them both. I told Zoe that this was an opportunity to be with Benji as he died and help him on his way. I told her she could hold his little paw and pray for his spiritual journey. While the other kids plundered the garden in an Easter egg hunt, Zoe set up her own palliative care unit. In a shoe box. She sat with Benji, weeping softly onto his fur. I went back to bed. It was awesome. Four hours later Benji died, the CD player churning the tired refrain to 'Get ready to wiggle'. Alas poor Benji, he would wiggle no more.

Zoe brought me his lifeless corpse, partially wrapped in the discarded Big Bunny foil from a half-eaten Easter egg. Sophia looked emotionless and unimpressed. As we lowered him into the hole I'd dug near the compost bin, Zoe started to sob again. She had learnt the lesson of Easter, where the Benji Jesus had died for our sins (well, to be honest, mine as I'd left the hutch open, but they didn't know that) and God please spare us the final resurrection. Nothing like an undead guinea pig for show and tell.

What little compassion Sophia had for her older sister was all but gone after the day-long ordeal. She looked at the sobbing Zoe in sheer disbelief and proclaimed, 'What are you so upset about … he only cost $7.50!' Thank God for economic rationalists and their relentless ability to move on. When it comes to grief, $7.50 doesn't even buy you a sob from my Sophia. For her, pet death is merely an unfortunate transaction that appears initially as a guinea pig deficit but later emerges as an opportunity to negotiate a larger, more expensive compensatory pet. 'Now Mum, what about that horse?' Vale Benji.

Hang on. That other guinea pig is not moving now.

# The morning of the Earth Mother

What I would do if I were you:
Not get out of bloody bed

Every morning I wake up and I think, *today, I am going to be a nice person*. But I can't do it. By 8 o'clock I have lost my mind. Of all the parenting challenges, it's the morning routine that turns my head inside out. Every day my kids act like the whole concept of getting up and going to school is a brand new idea. 'What? We're going to school? Really, what a surprise!' Whatever happened to the leisurely roll out of bed where one slipped on a silk chemise and padded into the kitchen for morning coffee? You'd sit at the kitchen table, the sunlight streaming across the laminex, clutching your steaming cup, still bleary eyed from the night of passionate lovemaking with your husband (or lover or bloke you picked up at the pub), who sits beside you rubbing your feet as he reads the paper. The two of you shower and dress for work, making vague arrangements for dinner. Then you pop on a bus and your day unravels.

Not for the breeding class. Morning is a spectacular display of aggression and endurance in the face of waning motivation where only those capable of precision performance under pressure win. In just 10 minutes of my feet touching floorboard, my pulse has risen from a calm 80 beats per minute to around 120. I may almost be having a heart attack, but at least I'm burning calories.

I have read all the parenting books about managing stress and understand the concept of keeping calm and rational. But honestly, I don't believe that parenting books are actually written by parents. If they are, the authors are know-it-all's with only one, over-functioning, compliant child. Parenting books aren't written by mothers of five dysfunctional children. If they were, they'd be suggesting that when it came to behaviour modification we use threats, fear and bribery. As for consistent parenting, every well-practised parent knows that inconsistency is the most effective of all techniques. It keeps the kids on their toes. Freak out when they spill water on the floor and then laugh it off when they let the hand brake off on the car and it ploughs into a tree. They'll never know what's coming next.

Lots of parenting books suggest 'morning meditation' as an effective way to manage a hectic schedule. I've tried it. It's bloody boring. I sat there cross-legged in my 'sacred space', which was actually a tea-stained rug in the lounge room littered with Lego.

My eyes were closed and I attempted to achieve 'no mind'. But all the unremembered tasks, odd jobs and miscellaneous details of the trillion meaningless things I needed to achieve each day filtered through my cortex in broken fragments: *Google how to remove tomato stains from white cotton, fill in permission note and scratch up $3 for swimming for Charlie, call the dog lady to trim Elvis, send a cheque to the lawnmower guy, book lip wax, buy jazz shoes for Sophia's upcoming dance recital, make another appointment for Zoe's psychologist and pick up her antibiotics, ring my mother, oh God, ring my grandmother. Shit, I don't have bread. Bloody hell. School lunches?* Any busy woman trying to achieve inner stillness will have this sensation.

These days I live in a state of constant sleep deprivation. My little Ivy has been known to wake 17 times in a night. They should use her at Guantanamo Bay. Even Osama Bin Laden would have buckled: 'I'll admit it. My secret identity is … Cat Stevens … and George Bush. I'm sorry, it wasn't an act of terrorism … it was a cry for help. Someone give me a hug!' Now that he's dead I can't help but suspect that he wasn't killed by US forces at all … it was Ivy.

Here's how a typical morning plays out in our house. At 5 a.m. Ivy calls. Well, screams, actually. I fetch her from her cot and then take her back to bed with John and I for another hour. I breastfeed her till the sun streams through the curtains. She sits bolt upright and says, 'Wiggies'. This is baby talk for *The Wiggles*. When it comes to language, babies are the ultimate minimalists. One word means a plethora of things. For instance, when Ivy grabs her shoes and says, 'Shoe shoe shoe', she doesn't just mean she wants her shoes on. What she is communicating is, 'It's boring in here, why don't we go out? Now.' Babies are semioticians. When she says, 'Wiggies' she means, 'Hey Mum, get your fat arse out of bed, go put *The Wiggles* on and make me some toast.'

It's 6 a.m. now. I'm in the lounge room. I still have half an hour before I need to wake Zoe. She gets a 7.20 a.m. bus and although she lopes around ironing her hair, complaining of feeling sick, not being able to find socks and vomiting after feeding the cat, she still manages to make it. Mostly. I'm on the couch having a cup of tea. Ivy is on her baby couch eating toast, kicking her legs and bouncing along to 'Big Red Car'.

We don't have a dishwasher. We actually have to wash up with our own hands. We're like cavemen in that way. None of the cave children want to do the dishes. I have photos of Sophia standing on a chair so she could wash up the cups. As a two-year-old, it was her favourite activity. If you ask her – or any of the others – to do the dishes now, they'll writhe and cry in emotional torment, 'Nooooooo, I did them last year.' Every few weeks I'll develop a program to encourage what I call 'cooperative' behaviour. It never works. None of them cooperate. So I am faced with the dishes from the night before piled on the bench. Usually they are spilling onto the kitchen table. A cockroach has met his maker in an uneaten mound of mashed potato. Fat has solidified in the frying pan. Ivy has thrown broccoli and rice all over the floor and pushed it into any recesses or cracks she can find. It's not something you want to face at 6.25 a.m. after just five hours of broken sleep. But there's nowhere else to prepare lunches. Perhaps I should tell them they're fat. Nothing like an eating disorder to cut back on lunch-making duties.

I want to cry. As my hands hit the sink I start to sulk and think, *Why aren't I living in luxury like all my rich friends? Why don't I have a dishwasher or a housecleaner or obedient children?* Then I remember: I don't have any rich friends.

It's 6.30 a.m. I push Zoe's door open to wake her and Rachel. A waft of pungent teenage girl stink hits me. It's a combination of putrid fishtank and rotten ugboot. Neither Zoe nor Rachel seem to mind. They think I keep their door closed to keep the baby out. I do it to keep the smell in. They share a large room with queen-size beds. This room-of-your-own business may have worked for Virginia Woolf and privileged little princesses, but in our house you share a room. The girls are pigs. They've piled so much crap on one of the beds that they've been forced to bunk in together. I worry that they'll be killed by an avalanche of discarded G-strings and shopping bags in the middle of the night.

They're both comatose. Zoe stirs, rolls over and mumbles, 'I feel sick.' Then she goes back to sleep. Yeah. Nice try. If I was to believe Zoe every time she said she was sick, she'd be on chemo. Sick is her default setting. She gives it a shot everyday on the off-chance that I'll weaken and let her stay home. I weaken about every two weeks, so her success rate is pretty high. She does actually look sick in the mornings as she's allergic to dust mites so her eyes are usually red raw and full of gunk. (We did get a call recently from her headmaster who was concerned she was smoking pot. I assured him the red eyes were from an allergy and that she is terrified of fire, so until she overcomes her fear of incendiary devices, she won't be puffing weed.) The smell of urine in the toilet also makes her vomit, so she does put on a good show when it comes to faking illness. She hates school. But she goes. Usually. Zoe's committed to doing as little as possible for as long as possible. However, when it comes to her physical appearance, Zoe's a contender for a scholarship. If hair ironing was an elective, she'd be an A student.

It's 6.35 a.m. I'm back at the sink working my way through the plates. The kettle is boiling. I wake Zoe and Rachel again. This time Zoe looks like she might be moving. I say the same sentence I say every morning, 'Hurry up Zoe, you'll miss the bus.' Like that concerns her. 'I hate that fucking school,' she grumbles. The potty-mouthed princess is up.

I scrape the frying pan and boil the kettle again. Time to wake Charlie and Sophia. In their bedroom I say, 'Come on, time to get up,' but nothing happens. I start begging. 'Come on, sweetheart, help Mummy, Mummy has a big day. Come on put your undies on. I'll hold them up. Put your foot through … come on!' I look around and see Sophia still asleep in her school uniform. Shit, Mummy was a bit pissed last night. Oh well, at least she's ready. Nothing like a good wipe down with a bit of spit and a chux cloth.

At 6.50 a.m. Rachel stumbles to the table. She wants to make toast. Except there isn't any bread. John's up and in the shower. Ivy is demanding a re-run of Wiggies. I know I shouldn't but it keeps her in the vicinity of the kitchen. Rachel watches her while I duck out to the shops. I'm wearing a giant T-shirt and thongs. In the bakery, as I queue behind the workmen ordering pies, I become aware that I'm not wearing any undies. It's not so you'd notice. It's just me knowing that my vagina is uncovered in a bread shop that's a little unsettling. I hope a pube doesn't decide now is a good time to leave the nest and drop on the tiles.

I'm home. It's 7a.m. now. There's movement at the station. I poke my head in to see Zoe. She's got a full face of make up. Her eyes are panda-ringed and her skin is as white as porcelain. She's ironing her hair. She's about half way through. But she's still in her pyjamas. 'Mum,' she says. 'You need to sign my Child Studies note.'

Always the last minute. I sign it. I don't even know what it says. The note could say, 'I give permission for my daughter to smoke bongs at lunchtime.' I'm under pressure. I don't sweat the details. This is usually the time the kids choose to make unrealistic requests, hoping that my poor brain function and lack of time will result in a positive response. 'Mum, can I go on the pill?' 'Can my boyfriend sleep the night?' ' Jaya's having a party, can I stay the weekend.' I use the Nancy Reagan approach and just say NO to everything. It saves thinking.

I dump the bread in the kitchen. Rachel makes toast. I boil the kettle again. This time I put two teabags in cups. The baby is bored of *The Wiggles* now and is attempting to put *Little Miss Sunshine* into the DVD player. It's keeping her busy, so I let her smear her grubby little peanut butter fingers all over the disc. It doesn't matter, it's not ours anyway, it belongs to the video shop. It's revenge for all the scratched DVDs they rent us.

The kettle boils and I finally make the tea. Zoe makes a beeline for the bathroom. You've got to be quick. We're a one-bathroom family, so when it comes to our mornings there's not a lot of gaps between a shit and a shave. Poor Charlie is forced to use his biological upper hand and pee in the yard. There's a shovel for number two's.

Charlie is now dressed and standing despondently at the pantry shelves. He's performing his daily audit on what he considers to be unimpressive supplies. 'What's for breakfast?'

'We have Weet Bix and Nutri-Grain.'

He's not sold. 'I hate Weet-Bix and Nutri-Grain.'

'Well, how about some toast?'

'I don't feel like toast.'

"Well, what if I make you pancakes with maple syrup?'

'Maple syrup makes me feel sick.'

'What if I cut you up a fruit salad?'

'I don't like fruit in the morning.'

'Well, what about baked beans on toast?'

'No, beans make me fart.'

I'm not sure what else to offer. While I'm an obliging mother, I'm not quite up to eggs Benedict at 7 in the morning.

'Dad has better breakfast at his house.'

I'm cut. I start making eggs Benedict. Beat that, Dad.

The dog is eating Ivy's toast. Actually, she's feeding it to him and letting him lick the peanut butter off the DVD. She's happy, so I don't interfere. It saves feeding him for a few hours. The cat is at the window. He's hungry. I can't hear him meow but I can see his mouth moving. I decide not to let him in. I just pull the blind so I don't have to witness his famished misery. I'll feed him later. Once the kids have gone.

It's 7.15 a.m. John's showered and dressed for work. I hand him his cup of tea but it's gone cold. He kisses Ivy, kisses me and then prepares to take Rachel back to her mother's house to get ready for school. She's still in her dressing gown. I watch them leave, envying the quiet simplicity of a car trip and a one-kid drop off.

Zoe is still not ready. She has to brush her teeth but she won't go back in the bathroom. 'Someone has done a shit in there and it stinks. I'll vomit.' You can't push her. She's a spewer.

'Brush your teeth in the kitchen sink.' I fetch the toothpaste and her brush. Being a mother I'm quite used to walking into fouled territory. It takes a lot to make me vomit. (Like my credit card bill.)

I don't bother making Zoe lunch. She'll only eat it if she buys from the canteen. According to her a cut lunch is embarrassing. I can't find any change so I have to give her $20. It's the only money I have. She looks delighted.

'Bye Mummy, I love you ...' Then she starts in with even more last minute requests. 'Oh, can you sign my planner ... tell them I couldn't do my history assignment due to family issues.'

There's no time to argue. I want her out the house. I sign the bogus note and she disappears. From the neck down she looks like a school girl; from the neck up, she looks like she's about to go to a nightclub.

Why do teenage girls wear so much make up? They're so beautiful as they are. It's the best anyone ever looks. Their foundation appears as though it was applied with a trowel, and according to most teenage girls, you just can't have enough eye liner. They want to look provocative and inappropriate. But instead of looking like beautiful 15-year-olds they look about 40. 'Slut' isn't an insult to them, it's a brand of lip gloss. *Lolita* has a lot to answer for.

Zoe has one last parting shot: 'Can you ring about me moving schools?'

'No.'

She slams the door. 'Fucking hate you.' It makes all the hard work worth it. When I pushed my eldest daughter into the world and held her to my breast and my heart swelled with love it was inconceivable that this same child would be at the front door saying, 'Fucking hate you.'

Ivy has taken her nappy off. She's playing with Big Baby, her life-size doll. She's happy. I leave her and start on the final shift: Sophia and Charlie. Their bus leaves in 30 minutes. Time for lunches. I want to cry.

I look around the kitchen. No lunchboxes. My heart starts to palpitate. I can feel the skin on my cheeks prickling. 'Where are your lunchboxes?'

I love the smell of lunch boxes in the morning....

I don't even know why I bother to ask. I know where they are. They're still in their bags. Every day after school I ask them to get their lunchboxes out of their bags. They don't even have to empty them. All they have to do is PUT them on the sink. But no, it can't be done. *I went to university to deal with their bloody lunchboxes.*

The lunchboxes come out. The lunches from yesterday are uneaten. I'm tempted to make them take the old lunches to school again. 'See, Mummy's gone green. She's recycling!' The untouched contents of the lunchbox make me feel like a failure. *What's wrong with my lunches? Aren't I good enough?*

Today I think, *bugger the diabetes statistics*, and pop in an iced donut, a packet of chips and a mango juice box. Sure, it's a lunch full of sugar and fat, but at least they'll eat it. When I have the shits with them I just stash a banana in their lunchboxes. It's a weapon of mass olfactory destruction.

Charlie is ready but he doesn't have his shoes on. He's frozen in front of the TV with Ivy. Their beds aren't made. Their pyjamas are on the floor. Sophia is fussing with her hair. In the last six months she's gone from being quite pretty to being a knockout. It's her last year at primary school and she intends to leave an impact. She's Amazon tall and has a new boyfriend every week. I chuckle when I see her standing next to this tiny boy whose head only comes up to her shoulder. She generally dumps them and moves on. She's ruthless.

Sophia was born tact impaired. She takes after my grandmother in that department. It's quite a skill. She's the master of rolling in a deftly planted insult that cuts right to the core. For example, poor Zoe's got pimples. Not a lot, but enough to affect her self-esteem. When Sophia spies her antibiotics in the fridge she will blurt out, 'Is that for your ACNE Zoe? Do you have ACNE?' Zoe will burst into tears and sob, 'You're such a bitch.'

Sophia will then look wide-eyed and say, 'What? I was just asking a question.' She'll smirk to herself and admire her perfectly tanned skin. Where Zoe has taken after her paternal grandmother and has skin of alabaster, Sophia is a throwback to my Viking heritage, her hair white blonde and her skin a constant honey caramel.

At 7.40 a.m. Sophia suddenly remembers that she has homework. This triggers Charlie's recollection about some 'talk' he was supposed to present. We have 10 minutes before the bus is due. Actually I have set the kitchen clock 15 minutes fast, so we have, in fact, 25 minutes. The fast clock gives me the illusion of more time. But it actually just creates more confusion as I'm constantly adding or subtracting 15 mins. One time my mother stayed and unbeknown to me, set the clock to the right time. It screwed my world. I spent the entire week running 15 minutes late.

While the kids are doing their homework I give a speech about being responsible and learning to plan your week.

'Mum, what's constitutional?'

'Which one is the numerator?'

I hate homework. I'm sure it's teacher's revenge. If they have to tolerate your snot-nosed DNA receptacle for the good part of each week, then it's only fair that you have to do a bit of the teaching. The clock is ticking down. Charlie still doesn't have his shoes on. Ivy's gone quiet. No doubt she's doing a poo. *God. Did I put a nappy on her yet?*

I fast-track the whole happy families scene by snatching the homework and doing it myself. Children may struggle to master the forgery of their parent's signature, but I've mastered my own children's scrawl. This new invention they call 'co-joined writing' is a joke. It's just printing with loopy bits. Whatever happened to proper handwriting, the thing we called running writing? Or learning times tables by rote? Both my teenage daughters couldn't answer 3 x 4. They're two fingers short. I was assured by a well-meaning principal that rote learning was a thing of the past, and that by Blu Tacking a poster of the times tables to the toilet door the kids would start to just assimilate the knowledge. It didn't work.

I deliver one of my famous 'when I was a kid' lectures. I feel the ancient lineage of mothers when I give this speech. It's like the voice of my mother, and my mother's mother is speaking through me. I'm a flesh puppet for the unheard words about tough childhoods and unappreciated privileges. The clock ticks over. It's bus time.

Suddenly there's movement. Children scramble for the toothbrush, grab lunchboxes, deposit homework books in the bag, find school hats. They run to the door. My heart is racing. I scoop up Ivy. She's covered in poo. No time to change her so I wrap her in a towel. We thunder down the front steps and the dog gets out. Charlie has to coax him back in. He manages to bail him up near the bins just as the bus flashes past. I'm furious. 'You've missed the bus!'

Magenta with rage I screech, 'Get in the car!' The children are ashen and silent. I bolt upstairs to clean Ivy. I stand her in the bath and wash the poo off her legs. She's so cute I can't be angry. She keeps saying, 'poo poo poo'. In just a few moments she has on a fresh nappy and, after a prima donna display in the frock department where every selection I suggest illicits a 'NO NO NO NO NO!', she is finally dressed in an ugly Dorothy the Dinosaur dress.

I strap Ivy into the station wagon. Charlie and Sophia are sitting quietly. 'Can I help you, Mummy?' they enquire.

Oh, now they're helpful. I'm still angry. I have to give one last speech. I've reached maximum despair. Men and children know what happens when women get like this. We need to rant. We need to tell you how you wrecked our lives. How it's never about us, and it's never my turn, and I hope when you grow up your children do this to you so you know what it's like. Give that speech in the house and they all rack off, but in the car, there's central locking. Sometimes when I'm having a particularly angst-ridden day and the kids are already at school, I'll consider picking up hitchhikers and scream at them, 'Look what you've done to me!' Not to frighten them necessarily but for the stress release.

I pull up in the 'No Stopping Zone' outside the school. Who are these parking restriction Nazis? The kids begin

complaining. 'Mum, you can't stop here, we get in trouble at assembly.' I think, *Oh yeah? Good.*

The kids hop out and start walking off. Then it happens. The mother guilt. It hits me like a psychic anvil. I'm crushed by the weight of my failure to be a nice person. It's weird. Kids up close are very irritating. But far away, they're heartbreaking. It's probably why farmers have such big families – keep 'em outside and you'll always love them. I'm flagellating now. I can't let them go like that. I beep the horn. They don't turn. I beep again. I see their little faces turn towards the car. They look despondent. Like, 'Oh no, the crazy bitch wants more.' I wave them over and they skulk up to the window.

'Mummy's sorry. Mummy's a bad mummy. I won't do it again. Don't tell your friends. I love you.'

Then I drive off. Once I get home I realise it's Saturday.

And I don't go back.

# The Incredible Sulk

I am a sulker. I can't help it. It's genetic. My grandfather had a profound sulk and didn't speak for 40 years. If there had been an Olympic event he'd be the Thorpie of the passive aggressive pool. He's part of our family legend. Norman Henry was my father's father. As a child I found him completely terrifying. Where my grandmother was fat, loud and affectionate, he was tall and thin with blazing blue eyes and as cold as a fish. Nanny had a maternal odour of talcum powder, sour milk and Vicks VapoRub. Pa smelt of rolling tobacco and dynamic lifter. I remember first seeing that classic painting, 'American Gothic', where a farming husband and wife clutch their pitchforks and stare coldly at the viewer. Pa could have sat for the portrait.

(Although he wasn't so much American Gothic as small country town Australian tragic.) He could have been Nick Cave's father.

No-one really knows why he stopped talking. Perhaps he had nothing to say. My grandmother, Ivy, who's 94 at the time of writing, never let on. Which was unusual because she generally never shut up. Legend has it he was a big drinker. Being Irish, he would have been an ideal candidate for a brand new alcoholic reality show called, 'So You Think You Can Drink'. My father would have taken the cup, or should I say tinnie, but sadly his spectacular career as a binge-drinking alcoholic was cut short when he was killed in a car accident at just 30. He was driving. Drunk, of course. Our 1973 powder blue Valiant became the portal for my dad to the next dimension.

Pa was about 20 years into his big sulk by this time and refused to attend the funeral. As an adult I have often wondered whether my grandfather's peculiar vow of silence was in fact the thing that drove my father to his early grave. That kind of silence is like cancer. You don't know how you got it exactly, but it's emotionally terminal. Every time I find myself pouting in cranky petulance I feel his quiet rage burning and think, *Christ, get over yourself.* The silent treatment is deadly. It drives people nuts. 'What's wrong?' you'll ask. 'Nothing', they reply. It's psychic violence. While it's illegal to assault your partner and you can be arrested for domestic violence, it should also be illegal to crack the shits. You can't see the bruises, but you can feel the impact of that kind of psychological torture for weeks. I want to see a government-funded health campaign which states, 'Warning: Passive Aggression Kills!'

I never loved my grandfather. I saw him every day of my childhood but I knew nothing about him. We had no relationship. He was less like a man and more like a stain. He didn't drink while I was growing up. I think if he had still been a pisshead, he might have been a lot more fun. At least he would have expressed emotion. He had a range of one: disinterested disconnection with a touch of disdain.

Unlike my dad, Pa dealt with his alcoholism. He stopped drinking completely. He didn't attend AA or rehab or watch 'Dr Phil'. He did it the old fashioned way. He took the part of his soul that was injured and nailed it shut. He nailed it so tight that not even a glimmer of light threatened to thaw that frozen heart. He locked himself in a bedroom for six weeks. My grandmother had the local Catholic priest praying for him outside the locked door but he refused to come out. With him bailed up in self-imposed exile, I imagine that was a very happy time for my grandmother and her children.

For six weeks, Pa pissed out the window and raided the pantry for supplies at night. God knows how he managed number two's. I don't think he showered. When he finally came out, he had a full Ned Kelly style beard. If it had been 'Movember' the man would have raised so much money he could have cured prostate cancer. This was the beginning of the incredible sulk. From the day he opened the door he didn't speak directly to my grandmother for 40 years. That's pretty impressive grudge holding. I've never managed more than a few hours and I'm a total bitch.

He did communicate to my grandmother in a roundabout sort of way. But it was always in the third person. He'd say, 'Tell her to make me a cup of tea.' And being the eternal diplomat, my kind and compassionate Nanny would respond directly with, 'You can take your tea and shove it up your arse.' This kind of response is what I love most about her. I used to wonder as a child just what she could have done to piss him off that much. Had she had an affair? Had she told him he had a small penis? Had she worn him down to a broken stump?

The cause was always speculative, as even now Nanny won't reveal what really happened, no matter how clever or thorough the cross examination. I was hoping she'd get dementia and spill the beans but the old girl is still as sharp as a tack. That conversation is now as closed as the door that took away Pa's speech. Sure, it was their relationship, they are entitled to privacy, but it's my family history. One dead father later I'd like to know. But in our family, that is a corpse buried so deep it will never be found. The rest of them aren't really talkers either. Maybe that's why I'm a comedian with a penchant for total and absolute public disclosure about every personal foible.

Pa had rules in his not talking. To conduct a proper verbal withdrawal and to sustain it you need to be able to function at a minimal level, while at the same time reminding everyone that you are a complete prick. He was a champion at it.

When he did speak (usually not more than one sentence every few weeks) his voice was so impersonal it sent shivers up your spine. He was also a minimalist. He didn't say hello. Or goodbye. Or thank you or please or use your name. That was all far too personal. He would just blurt out a random statement like, 'roof needs fixing' and move on. This made the telephone extremely confronting. As an eight-year-old I remember ringing my grandmother's house and after about 30 rings Pa picked up. Telephones are very hard to answer without 'hello'. So there was this long silence, punctuated by the wheeze of his emphysema and finally a single rasped word: 'telephone'. It was frightening.

I thought that everyone had a grandfather like him. My mother's father died before I was born so he was my only experience of a granddad. I had no idea that they could be loving, kindly men who laughed and played and actually enjoyed the company of children. I'd only seen those kinds of grandfathers in Christian TV ads. I was more inclined to think grandfathers were ghouls who stared so deeply at you that they could steal your soul. Watching a Harry Potter movie with my kids, I was shocked how similar Pa was to the evil wizard Voldemort. Pa stared at me the same way Voldemort stared at Harry. (Although he was more weirdo than wizard.) In fact, I was five before I realised he was even related to me. I thought the man who lurked like a dark shadow in the backyard was the gardener.

His complete withdrawal into his peculiar internal world had left him with very strange characteristics. He was antisocial, yet still creative, in a spooky kind of way. He loved raiding the tip and so had an endless supply of bottles at his disposal, and then somehow he got his hands on a Demtel glasscutter. I'll never forget the Gaudi-like matching candleholders he fashioned from the beer bottles. They stood at least six feet high and had to be fixed to the wall in the dining room with leather straps.

Then there was the fungal phase. One summer Pa developed a technique for making concrete mushrooms. He would pour concrete into makeshift moulds of dishes and lids to form the mushie caps. He'd fashion stalks from hoses, or mini concrete pylons. Then he'd paint giant orange spots on them. I once counted how many there were. I made it to 53. All of various sizes and functions. Some were purely decorative, lining the edges of garden beds, and others were functional and used as mushroom seats.

The pièce de résistance of his fungal formations was the 12-seat BBQ setting.

Twelve large mushroom seats were created and placed in a 'fairy ring' around a giant pink and green mushroom, which acted as the BBQ. It was so ugly and so enormous, it was breathtaking. It was the Nolan family's Stonehenge, replete with druid.

As a child, I loved having a mushie barbie. Of course, Pa never attended any of these events. My boyfriend and I once visited Nanny in my early twenties after smoking a huge joint. I'd warned my boyfriend: 'Don't go in the back yard, you'll lose it.' But sure enough, he went and when he was confronted with

the mushroom BBQ setting he laughed so hard he collapsed onto the lawn, where he remained in a foetal position giggling for almost an hour. 'It's like a Diane Arbus photograph,' he gasped.

As he laughed I was confronted by the irony of it all. It was one of those deep revelations you have only when you are stoned. Here was a man who had sulked for four decades, yet toiled for months to construct a communal eating facility that he would never sit at. I cried the only tear I ever cried for him. And it was just one.

To not talk for a day takes perseverance. To not talk for a week takes bloody mindedness. To not talk for four decades takes a certain kind of madness. Perhaps Pa had such a delicate touch with concrete because he was made of concrete himself. He was immovable.

One day I was helping Nanny clean up after lunch. Pa wouldn't sit with his family and always ate when everyone had left the table. This particular day he came in from the garden and sat at the table. He still had his Akubra hat on. He never took it off. As a child I thought he slept in it. Nanny pushed his ham salad in front of him and then went to pour a glass of orange juice. But instead of pouring the juice into the glass she turned and poured the entire contents of the 2-litre container onto Pa's head. Thank God he was wearing his hat. It pooled in the crown and then became juicy waterfalls flowing over the brim, and running down his beard, his neck, his shirt and his trousers. He even had juice in his food.

There was complete silence in the kitchen. I was frozen at the sink. Nanny just said, 'Whoops' and kept pouring. Pa didn't move. He suffered his juice bath in silence. Then there was that quiet bit, like the eye of a cyclone. No-one moved. No-one said anything. Pa picked up his knife. I began to panic, thinking, *He's going to kill my nanny. And then me.* Instead, he picked up his fork and ate his ham salad, which was now an orange juice soup. After he finished he rolled a cigarette and had a cup of tea while reading his orange juice-soaked newspaper. Exactly 22 minutes after sitting (his usual time) he stood up. More juice poured off him onto the floor. He walked slowly to his bedroom and closed the door. That was when I first realised he was dead. He was later diagnosed as having the worst case of clinical depression the doctor had ever seen.

And then, just as suddenly as he stopped, he started speaking again. Apparently, something had happened to Pa. He thawed, ever so slightly. Occasionally he'd twist his lips into this weird shape, which I think was a smile. He suddenly appeared vulnerable.

I don't think Pa started talking because he'd had an emotional epiphany. You don't just back down from a lifetime behaviour like that. I think he'd got dementia and actually forgotten that he wasn't supposed to be talking.

My grandmother was stoic after her 40 years in the emotional desert. This Moses of a woman had reached the promised land of a communicative husband but she wasn't impressed. He started talking one day about the weather and she snapped,

'For God's sake we don't want to hear about the weather, it's boring.' She told me later that she preferred it when he didn't talk. Too much had happened to suddenly let go and pretend it was all nice.

So after a fight with John, when I'm holed up in my room contemplating never coming out, I wonder how much of my genetic code is shared with this man who didn't speak. I start the emotional shut down. I throw the switches. I feel the slide into sulk. I get a sudden compulsion to fashion mushrooms from risotto. Then I'm out into the arms of my man. 'I'm sorry, I was wrong.' He holds me and then pushes me back a little for a closer inspection.

'Mandy, I think you're growing a beard!'

# Sack my cook

Every afternoon, everywhere in the world, mothers release a collective groan of 'Bloody dinner'. While I recognise that men do cook, traditionally it's a 'special event' that requires a cheer squad, an impromptu poem of gratitude and a documentary crew. Generally when it hits 6 p.m. it's us girls who are standing at the stove while the blokes are winding down with a beer. I find I have to start thinking about dinner at breakfast. It's really hard trying to envisage what you're going to eat that night when you're munching on peanut butter toast and sipping your first cuppa. It's not really when I want to be thinking about meat.

Coming up with dinner every night is like working for a catering company with a high-needs group. I have to assess how many bodies are going to be at the table and their particular dietary persuasions. Some nights it's just John and I, Zoe and the baby. Other nights we have the whole crew. The meal that delights one child brings misery to the other. Charlie and Rachel absolutely love fish. Zoe hates it. Sophia loves mashed potato. Charlie hates it. So does the baby. Rachel would live only on bacon. So would the rest of the kids. John too. But I have high cholesterol. Charlie loves butter chicken but Zoe thinks it's too spicy. They will only eat white bread. Zoe and Rachel and Sophia love the bread with the sesame seed crust. Charlie says it makes him sick. The only vegetable they'll all eat is broccoli. None of them will eat tomato. Unless it's cooked.

The only meals we have consensus on are lasagne and spaghetti bolognese. But I'm Mrs Fatty and supposed to be eating low carb. Basically that means the dog and I are sitting down to a bowl of mince.

Zoe has recently decided that she's gluten intolerant. I've discovered that I also have a dietary problem. I'm gluten intolerant intolerant. When I see people buying gluten intolerant products I want to scream at them, 'Get your special $10 rock-hard bread, get in the car, and go home!' Until a few years ago people didn't even know what gluten was. Now they can't tolerate it.

'Gluten free' has become the marketing tag of products that never contained gluten in the first place. I've picked up a packet of high-salt, high-fat potato chips which cheerily claims its 'gluten free' like it's frickin' health food!

These days you're really not part of the human food chain if you don't have a food intolerance. Celiac, gluten free, lactose intolerant, allergic to nuts …

When I was a kid you didn't make a fuss. You ate what you were given and you shut your mouth. Oh yeah, sure, there was the odd person who swelled up or got itchy, and occasionally someone died, but at least we bred them out. Now they're everywhere. Even me. A recent blood test revealed that I really am gluten intolerant. Bugger that for a joke, there's no love in gluten-free bread. I'm staying on my crusty rolls. Who cares about the pelvic bloating? I think it's charming to permanently look three months pregnant. People are always telling me I'm glowing.

Until I had kids I had no idea what a challenge it is to devise a menu that everyone would eat. I suddenly realised the monotony of deciding what to cook for dinner is what sends women mad. Life is what happens to you between the lunch box and the evening meal. My ex-husband Russ was an extraordinary cook. When we were together, I lived like a man. I don't mean that I left the toilet seat up and farted in public (I always do that). I mean that I probably only cooked four meals during our entire relationship. I would be at home with three kids under six, Russ would be out working 16-hour days on a film shoot and I'd ring him asking, 'What's for dinner? I'm hungry.' I had the decency to fetch the ingredients, but the poor bastard would walk in the door at 7 p.m. straight into food preparation for his starving family.

I loved his cooking. He'd prepare won ton soup, and make all the won tons himself. His chicken would be lightly dusted in turmeric, his vegetables all sautéed to perfection. He had this ability to create meals with such delicate fragrances that I lost all cooking confidence. In comparison, my food was burnt and over flavoured. The kids wouldn't eat it. In the end I couldn't even manage to heat up a can of beans. When Russ and I separated I had to learn to cook again lest my children request to live full time with their father. Damn, at dinner time, I wanted Russ to be my dad too.

I remember preparing a meal for John in the early days of our relationship. It was at that stage when I still wanted to impress him. That early phase when you are still creating the picture of who you are for your partner. In advertising, they call it the 'sell'. If what I presented was to be believed, I was quite a catch. Compassionate, funny, stylish, selfless, artistic, a devoted mummy, a talented homemaker, an exercise fiend and sexual vixen; I was something else. Even if I was accompanied by my three assorted genetic accoutrements.

Turns out I was really a self-absorbed, lazy, deluded, controlling, attention-seeking slob who couldn't fry an egg. (However, I really was a sexual vixen. I think that's why John stayed.) So I made John a lamb roast. I know the way to a man's heart is with a lump of meat. I busted out the only *Marie Clare* cookbook I had left since the divorce. I was lucky Russ left it. It wasn't even mine in the first place. I think he left it out of pity, or maybe it was to remind me of what I'd lost.

I sat the lamb on a wire rack, hovering above a tray of water. I studded the outside with garlic and rosemary sprigs and basted it with a honey mustard dressing. It smelled amazing. For the first time ever I managed not only to get the vegetables crispy, but they reached their culinary climax at the same time as the meat. When John arrived, the entire house smelled of roast lamb. I could see the desire in his eyes. It was primitive. It was visceral. It was working!

I pulled the lamb out of the oven. There was a strange smell when I opened the oven door. I couldn't quite identify it as I had never used the oven independently. I assumed it was an oven smell. As I began to serve up I thought, *I don't remember adding eggplant. Hang on. That's not eggplant. That black charred substance is ... the meat pad!* In my näive attempts to impress my new man with a sumptuous chunk of lamb flesh, I had forgotten to remove the meat pad. The entire oven reeked of burnt plastic. I had not only cooked a lamb roast with a honey mustard crust, I'd added my own toxic glaze. Bet *Marie Clare* hasn't got that recipe in its index.

John's look of admiration and desire turned swiftly to disappointment. His erection subsided as I deposited the lamb and her perfectly roasted vegetables into the bin. We ordered a pizza. 'This is who I really am,' I confessed. I so wanted to be that other woman. The one that can cook. When you're middle aged and too lazy to be anorexic, you figure out that cooking is not some boring chore; it can be sexy.

It's not the first time. I've disappointed many men with my poor culinary ability. In my early 20s when I was still at uni, I had a love interest over for dinner. Of course, we were vegetarians then, so I made a cheesy pasta. I was an anarchist at the time and believed the recipes were unnecessarily restrictive and too focused on rules. So I made it up myself. I boiled pasta, and when it was cooked I drained most of the water and added a thick yellow glob of cheese. It looked like some nasty bowel obstruction. To his credit my friend ate the meal, albeit slowly, with a lot of facial expression. He said nothing for a few minutes and then broke the silence with the comment, 'I'll say one thing Mandy, you can't cook, but you make a fine glue!' I fell in love with him straight away. He soon left me for a girl who ran a macrobiotic cooking class.

So at 43 I decided it was time to lift my game. I didn't want to hide my head in shame at the dinners where my gastronomically gifted girlfriends coo, 'bring a plate'. I didn't want my sad plate of Jatz topped with Coon and gherkin to sit next to the ravioli in garden fresh pesto or olive oil drizzled bruchetta with homemade anchovy paste. Rather than working on my abs, I started working on my kitchen fitness. I bought cookbooks and I sat down with a cup of tea and read them. I attempted the easier recipes. I actually followed the instructions. I learned that the secret to being able to cook is planning. Part of my long-term cooking failure was that I didn't think about it until 7 p.m. and then I wouldn't have a clue so I'd just boil some rice and up-end a can of tuna. I started writing meal plans and creating shopping lists that included ingredients required for our weekly menu. Suddenly, supermarkets didn't confuse me

any more. When I went in there I knew exactly what I wanted. I had a list. For the first time ever I felt like a real woman. I had found my C spot!

Only problem is, now I'm cooking, I'm not so interested in fucking. Maybe instead of food being a sex substitute, it's the opposite! Maybe we only fuck like rabbits when we don't know how to cook them.

I have a friend who is into raw food. Well, she dresses it up with a fancy nutritional name but basically she just stopped cooking altogether. Her family eat fruit, vegetables and the odd bit of salmon. The stove is only used for lighting her rollies when the kids have gone to bed. They live like gorillas. No one sits down to eat any more, they just scavenge around the lounge room looking for bananas. I just couldn't live like that. Not only have I started to enjoy cooking, I love our meal times. When John came into our family he only insisted on one thing: that every night we come to the table and eat together. The TV is turned off. Telephones aren't answered. There's no music on. We sit and eat and talk. At first the kids hated it. They screamed in defiance. They swore at us. Now, on some nights we'll sit around the table for two hours talking and laughing. The kitchen table is the place where we come together. Sharing a meal connects us. I just don't think you get the same buzz off a fruit salad.

# Five little ducks went out one day

Being a parent is terrifiying. The moment my cervix dilated 10 centimetres and a brand new human being emerged, I opened the door to a world of anxiety that I never knew existed. Prior to becoming a parent I'd driven drunk, smoked pot and swum naked in shark-infested waters while smeared in dog food. I communed with un-immunised hippies and lived in a shed with a snake in the roof and a mattress on the floor.

Having babies changed the way I saw the world. Where before I'd looked around and seen a cosy room, I suddenly saw sharp corners, poisonous chemicals, gaping doors and finger-mashing cupboards. Glorious sun-soaked decks became a place where a child could push a chair to the edge and fall to their death, a crystal clear plunge pool was an opportunity to drown at home and the ingenious straightening magic of the hair iron became a device for toasting small tongues.

Anxiety about my kids keeps me awake at night. What if I totally fuck them up? What if they turn out to be stupid? Maybe I don't do enough after school activities. Maybe I need to get more involved in their school. But there's a problem with that one. I hate getting involved in the school stuff. I always feel so ostracised by the super mum squad. You know, the team of full-time mums who do all the guided reading, uniform shop, canteen, fundraising and netball coaching stuff. These are the mums that come to every assembly. The mums that hand every note in on time. They know everything. They stand in huddles at kiddie pick-up chatting to each other, sharing their secret mum business. It's not a social group you can just break into. These are the Chummy Mummies. Every time I approach them, they stop talking until I leave. Their kids are always getting awards. They win citizenship ribbons, maths medals, they come first in the 100 metres, make it to State for school sport.

I've never known the thrill of my kids winning stuff. My kids are so secure they've never felt the need to be over-achievers. Perhaps I should start putting them down more. Start withholding love. Hopefully with a bit of low self-worth they'll be re-invigorated with a desire to prove themselves and start achieving. Next time I have to attend one of those dreary sporting carnivals I might try saying, 'I didn't come all the way to watch you come fourth, loser.' Hang on, I already did that.

There's a lot of pressure on parents to allow their children 'freedom'. It gives me panic attacks. I am not one of those drop-your-kids-at-the-beach-and-let-them-go-surfing-and-find-their-own-way-home type mums. I'm a breastfeed-until-they're-in-kindergarten type of mum who worries incessantly about child mortality. If I could pop the titty into the lunchbox I would. I like to think of my children as tethered by a long invisible chain of love that's attached to a stake driven hard into the ground. That stake is me. And they will never escape.

I hate my children going anywhere. I am suspicious of new environments. I don't trust other parents. Why should I? Until proven otherwise I assume they are crack-smoking bikies who will allow them to watch R-rated movies like *Wolf Creek* while feeding them McDonalds and beating them with a stick. Every time my child befriends a new kid who asks them over to play I conduct an informal survey to establish whether or not I am sending my child to the home of serial killers. You need to mask your questions otherwise the other parents become defensive and your child will become a social outcast. So I usually shoot off a few harmless queries such as, 'Have you ever been arrested? Do you have permission from police to work with children? Would you mind giving me your full name so I can run a quick police check?' Assuming that's all good I then say, 'Charlie would love to come over to play. Next year. Once I've done a health and safety inspection of your premises.'

Having kids is killing me. I live in a constant state of high alert. The world is dangerous. I am reminded of this while driving when I see three tiny shapes moving onto the bitumen. A brown mother duck has decided that 11 a.m. on a rainy Saturday is a great time to cross the highway with her two little fluffy ducklings. This storybook scene unfolds in the middle of an 100 kilometre per hour death trap. I hit the brakes. If I ran over a mother duck and her ducklings I don't think I'd ever come out of counselling. Jesus, is there a DOCS for ducks? What the hell was she thinking? You don't take your babies across a road. Surely whatever is on the other side is not worth being mowed down by an approaching vehicle! Fortunately mumma duck makes it across. This time. I am so moved by the fragility of life that I start to cry. My daughter Sophia, who is sitting in the passenger seat, looks at me like I'm nuts. I probably am. If I run over the ducks I cry. If I don't run over the ducks I cry. I think that I am that mother duck – and every day I must send my most precious ducklings into a world that may not return them.

When I send my kids down the street to buy milk I warn them about creepy pedophiles with fluffy puppies. I warn them to be careful crossing the road, and not to use the pedestrian crossing because they are more dangerous than jay walking. I tell them not to lick the receivers of public telephones because they're covered in hepatitis, that you don't sit on a public toilet seat because someone else's wee could touch your bum or you could get bum germs and catch herpes or festering butt sores. Don't drink water in plastic bottles that have been in the sun because you'll get cancer, don't eat margarine because you'll go blind, don't eat sugar because you'll get diabetes or fat or cancer or both, don't make friends with weirdos on Facebook in case they stalk you then meet you at a train station and murder you.

My eldest daughter Zoe pipes up at the dinner table one night, 'You know what's rude?' I am struck by her sudden interest in etiquette.

'No, darling, what is rude?'

'When people rape you and THEN murder you.'

I'm dumbfounded, both by Zoe's statement and the truthfulness of it. Choose one or the other, but to do both is just plain greedy, Mr Raping Murderer. I can't even pretend to think like Zoe! It scares me that she's so desensitised to the concept of violence that she thinks there should be a code of etiquette attached to it.

Other warnings I issue include don't put buttons or foreign objects in your mouth because you'll choke. (Teenage girls take note, that also goes for penises.) Don't get immunised, you could end up with a disability. Get immunised, it will stop you ending up with a disability or a nasty case of whooping cough, or falling down dead from diptheria or tetanus or polio. Bang on the back steps before you walk down them because brown snakes live under the house. Don't eat unwashed lettuce because you'll get botulism. Don't talk on the mobile for too long because you'll get a brain tumour. Don't wear an underwire bra while you're on the computer because it will radiate your boobs and give you breast cancer. Don't eat burnt toast. Don't stick your fingers in mysterious holes. (Teenage boys take note.) Don't lick

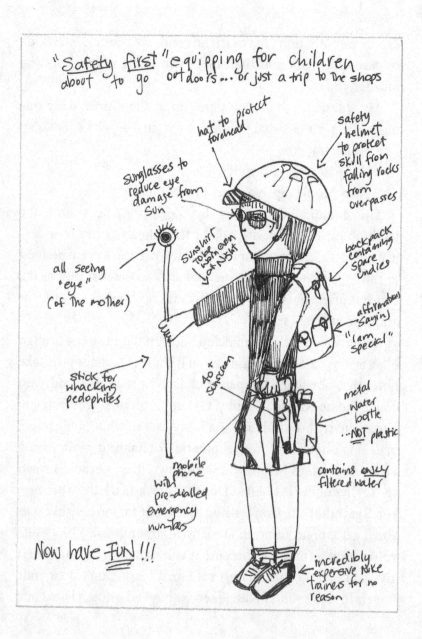

leaking batteries. Don't ride your bike. Don't swim in estuaries, they all contain some weird flesh-eating bacteria. Don't hit people with a cricket bat. Don't wear polyester, it gives you a nasty rash. Don't use public showers without wearing thongs, you'll get planta warts. Don't get in the car with stoners. Don't hitchhike or you could get picked up by some out of control psychopath. If you are driving, don't pick up hitchhikers; they could be out of control psychopaths. Don't take drugs (like I did). Don't drink. Don't smoke. And you know what, just don't drive, there's nowhere really worth going anyway. Just stay at home. With me. Until you're 40. And no-one wants you. It will be just you and your mum. There's nothing creepy about that.

I can't get the ducklings out of my head. I'm worrying about them every day. I can't sleep for thinking of all the mothers who don't get their ducklings across the road. It's the absolute powerlessness of it that frightens me. One morning at 3 a.m. in an insomniac stupor I get in the car. I drive to the grassy knoll by the highway. I wait. Mumma duck emerges from the reeds with her babies. I bag them, chuck them in the boot and drive them home. I lock them safely in the bathroom. I fall asleep. I wake to a scream of a child wandering to the loo for a morning pee. 'Mum! I've been attacked ... by a duck!'

# You're driving me crazy

The car was intended to be a vehicle of liberation. When it comes to realising the heady goals of the cult of individualism you could say that the car was the iPhone of last century. myCar.

I wish I'd never learnt to drive. I hate it. Ever since my first 10-centimetre dilation I've been on the road. I don't think I've been out of the car in 15 years. (Of course, I pop into the back seat occasionally to give birth.) I'm not just a mother. I'm a frickin' taxi. I spend so much time in the driver's seat that if you filled its crevices with plaster of Paris, you'd get an exact mould of my fat arse.

I drive kids to soccer, I pick them up. I drive Charlie to his friend's house for a sleepover. I get a call at 10 p.m. that my son is feeling 'sick' so I pick him up. Turns out he was just a bit sooky for Mummy. (My daughters were ready to cut the parental ties as soon as we cut their umbilical cords, but my son is far softer, more needy of the affection and routine of his own home. He'll be living at home until he's 30.) I drive Zoe to see her boyfriend. I meet the boyfriend's mother half way. The two of us stand in our track pants, slumped against our driver doors like poorly dressed chauffeurs, waiting for the love struck teens to remove their tongues from each other's tonsils. I drive to drums. I drive to take the overdue DVDs back. I drive to the shops. I drive to work. I drive to school. I pick up kids. I drop kids off.

I'm not alone. Zombie drivers are everywhere. I recognise that dead-eyed stare as they cut me off and steal the only vacant park outside the building where my daughter is taking a dance class. I pull into the disabled spot and put my hazard lights on. I may not have a handicap sticker but I do have psoriasis and an ingrown toenail. Honestly, what's the chance of a disabled person turning up at a dance class? I release the seat and stretch back for a nap.

These are the commitments that kill me. Forty-five minutes is too short a time to get your bikini line waxed or have an affair so I slump against the wheel for a micro-snooze. Suddenly there's a tap at the window. A very pissed off woman eyeballs me. *Jesus, she's a midget!* Then I realise she's in a wheelchair. She has had

to park on the footpath. Somehow she's managed to negotiate her massive disabled vehicle over the gutter. How embarrassing. I apologise. I blurt out the first thing that comes into my head. 'I'm sorry … just had a new windscreen put in and they haven't issued my new sticker!' I'm disgusted with myself.

The woman eyes the giant stone chip on the passenger side of my windscreen and shakes her head. She wheels off with a 'Fuck you.' I respond appropriately with a 'Fuck you too.' Then I realise I've just abused a disabled person. After stealing her park. That's got to be a red flag. I really have to stop driving. I'm going nuts. I think I've developed a kind of car-borne mental health issue.

I've become one of those women with a big car full of kids. And the car's not sexy. I'm not talking your regular five-seater. I'm talking the seven-berth mover. It's a car that screams, 'That woman's got no sperm filter.' That's right, environmentally aware population control Nazis, I am destroying the universe, one reverse park at a time. And if you've seen how I drive, watch out. There's going to be paint scrapes on Uranus.

When I reverse I don't bother looking. It's not that I can't. It's just that I'm tired and as far as I'm concerned it's just one more job. Generally there's no one in the cars that I hit, and usually it's such a tiny ding that I feel quite justified in driving off. It doesn't seem to worry anyone. In fact, when it happened last week, the woman driver waved. It was obvious, at least to me, that we had some of deep 'connnection'. Either that or she was using sign language to indicate that I was Number One.

A friend of mine said recently, 'Mandy, you have to stop attracting all this conflict into your life.' Then she handed me a copy of the book called *The Secret*. If I had been in my car I would have driven over her.

I hate *The Secret*. I think it's immoral. It's based on the law of attraction. Just because you've been a guest on *Oprah*, doesn't mean you can just go around making up laws for the universe. The law of gravity and the law of motion are real scientific laws, but the law of attraction? It sounds like something Guthy Renker would sell at $49.95 per month.

In my opinion, *The Secret* was written by a moron for morons. So if you are into it, I'd take the title as a hint and keep it secret. It's basically just an elaborate justification for privileged people to feel they have no responsibility to alleviate the suffering of others. In a nutshell, (and *Secret* followers are nuts and should stay in their shells), if I am living in a hole in Ethiopia with not even a goat to my name, well, that's not because of civil war or the unfair distribution of wealth. It's because I believed I was poor and unworthy and created that dismal reality. However, if I am living in a mansion in Bellevue Hill then whacko, I am a genius, because I created it with my positive and powerful thinking! It had nothing to do with the generations of wealth I inherited from mining tycoons who may or may not have profited through the misery of others.

Anyway, I'm reverse parking and I hit this car. It's a pretty big hit. (You know it's big when your airbag inflates.) I release myself by puncturing the airbag with my nailfile and approach the woman driver sitting in the Mercedes, which is now sporting a handsome red paint smear on its buckled fender. It looks like the silver Merc is wearing lipstick. I can see the woman is fuming. Even though her head has been frozen stiff with botox, I can tell she's angry by the way the dribble is catching in the corners of her mouth. She zaps down her electronic window and I catch sight of a book lying on the passenger seat. It's a copy of *The Secret*. 'You hit me!' she snarls.

I can't help myself. 'Yes, I was just wondering what you did to make that happen.' Botox starts foaming out of her ears. This comment cost me over $2000 but was well worth it.

So if you can't reverse, get a big car. It was never my intention but I've become quite fond of my boxy people mover. I'm going to keep breeding until I can fill a mini-bus. I've become what I once feared: a woman in a van full of ankle biters. You see a woman like that and you think, I am not going to fuck with her. She could go postal.

When I'm driving I like to use the rear vision mirror to check the kids. Not to see if they're wearing seat belts or unfastening doors, but just to marvel at the sheer wonderment of my very own human zoo. I made all those people. It's like human playdough. There must be a carbon cloud a mile thick above my van. It's not a footprint any more, it's a whole bloody leg.

Ironically it was the cops who were to become my driving salvation. I got picked up for speeding. It wasn't the first time. Or the second. Or the third. My licence mirrored my life ... it was totally pointless. I was already on a good behaviour bond. Like that was going to work!

I'd just finished this gig in Armidale. I was pregnant with Ivy at the time and I had Charlie, Zoe and Sophia in the car with me. It was 7 a.m. and I was hurtling along the highway doing some classic driving parenting: 'Zoe, stop hassling Charlie. For God's sake, if I have to come back there ...' A blue light flashed past, requesting that I pull over. Mr Tight Pants highway-patrol man informs me that I was doing 120 km in 100 km zone. All I can say is, 'Correct.' He asks why am I exceeding the speed limit? I tell him I'm leaving Armidale. Surely that's reason enough?

Then I did something I'm not proud of. Something shameful. I started to cry. Not just cry, but blubber, choking out long drawn out salty gasps as water literally leaks out of my head. 'Please ... if, if, if you book me ... I'll lose my licence ... I'm on a good behaviour bond ... and I live in a small town ... with three kids ... and I'm pregnant.' The bastard booked me on the spot. I should have retained my dignity and offered him a blow job instead. My kids thought it was hysterical and spent the rest of the trip imitating me crying and begging with the cop.

So I lost my licence. For six months. It was incredible. I don't think I've ever been so happy. I had a four-wheeled epiphany. It is possible to live without a car. Of course, it's not possible though, to live without someone else's car. I became the master of what I call 'lift negotiation' which was really just manipulating other people into driving me somewhere. It was exactly like being a teenager.

I even paid a friend to drive me to gigs so I didn't wear my husband out entirely. And what a nightmare that was! As we're pulling out of the drive she reminded me of her roadworthy status. 'Don't worry, I haven't smoked a joint for three hours.'

A few minutes later after riding the clutch, stalling and over steering, she apologised. 'I'm sorry, I don't usually drive at night. I get night blindness and I can't see.' Wow, stoned and blind. And I'm the one who lost their licence!

I even gave hitching a go. Well, the first time it wasn't really hitching. A woman stopped her car at a pedestrian crossing and I just got in and told her to drive me home. Actually hitching wasn't really viable with four kids and an infant. Every car that stopped I had to ask, 'Do you have a bolt for a baby seat?' Then I'd spend the next 20 minutes trying to get the baby seat in a stranger's car.

There were weeks when I didn't leave home at all. They were the weeks when I really let myself go. It was glorious. I have to admit I had this delicious glow of smugness. For the first time in over two decades of holding a licence I was truly green. I was using public transport. I was so in love with myself I had 'I get the bus' printed on T-shirts. I was queen of the loser cruiser.

On the other hand I felt like a complete tosspot, reduced to pushing my grocery laden pram through bushland, while dragging weeping children and copping abuse from passing teenagers. (Being on foot, one is much more susceptible to random abuse – you are a much slower moving target. One particular day three scrawny weed-dealing emo boys ran past

and yelled, 'Mandy Nolan's a slut'. How did they know? Their teacher must have talked.)

The kids no longer had after-school activities. We couldn't visit people and I couldn't do the weekly big shop (although that was bliss). After my six-month sabbatical I thought that being back behind the wheel would bring me an euphoric sense of freedom akin to the characters from a Herman Hesse novel. Instead I sat in the driver's seat and wept. My half year of being public transport and partner dependent had enlightened me. True freedom is in *not* driving. The car is a prison that creates the illusion of freedom, but is in itself nothing but a fast moving metal cage. In the six months of home detention I shopped, I played and I worked all within walking distance of my home.

I had become a reluctant environmentalist. I did not buy more than I could carry. I could balance my decaf latte on my head, push a pram full of sundries with my hip while breastfeeding my infant and chatting on my iPhone. I was just like a Third World mother!

Not having a licence meant that I played with my baby, I started writing a book, I painted an exhibition and I cleaned. One day my husband came home and all his shirts were ironed. He had an instant erection. I worked on a film script. I read some books. I wrote plays with the kids and acted them out instead of watching TV. I meditated. I took up piano (which was made more difficult by not actually owning one but my new meditation skills meant I simply manifested one whenever

I needed to practise). I did my own waxing. (My husband lost his erection.) I grew vegetables. (Great erection substitutes.) I made jam. Every night I prepared meals from my *Marie Claire* cookbook. I always washed the vegetables. I crocheted around the tea towels. I even started felting (using recycled hair from my attempts at the home brazilian). I owe a debt of gratitude to the Roads and Traffic Authority for getting me out of the driver's seat and back into my life. I may have lost my licence; but I got my life back.

To those of you living behind the wheel: put down the keys and take back your life. Every time you turn that ignition switch you are going nowhere.

# This is not a love thong

After almost three decades of fertility I have finally found the perfect contraception that's free from side-effects. In the past I've tried the pill and consequently put on weight, grew a beard and got angry. It was pretty effective. I didn't get pregnant. Mainly because I didn't have sex. No-one wants to bonk an angry, fat, female Rolf Harris. I then tried using a diaphram. But I can't hold my breath for longer than one minute. I even used an IUD. It didn't work that well as contraception but it was the first time I was able to get SBS. So then I tried the humble caravan park. For those of you rushing to book your triple berther, let me give you fair warning: as a contraceptive, it's so effective you may never have sex again.

Holidays with a big family are always a challenge. When I had one kid it was a doddle. I'd ring up a friend, grab a plane and spend a week on their couch or in the spare room. Budget relaxation at someone else's expense. However, once you've got a sizeable family it's pretty near impossible to find anyone who's willing to accommodate you for an afternoon, let alone an entire night. And as for jumping on a plane, when you have to fork out seven airfares it makes that cheap and cheerful weekend another unwelcome cash hemorrhage. And as for driving, anything more than an hour away is not a holiday. It's a seven-seat car journey straight to hell.

When big families phone their friends for a favour, no-one answers. You're left smack bang in hotel territory. But you can't just book one room. Fire regulations state that for a family of our size it's a three-bedroom minimum. If you're going to burn to death it's going to be no more than two to a room. Makes identifying the bodies so much easier. Fortunately no such regulation applies to caravans. The human rights convention stops where the van park begins. When it comes to caravans, the more people you can fit in a 10-metre square space the better. After sitting on the couch and sulking that we couldn't afford a five-star hotel on Sydney Harbour, I started warming to the concept of metal confinement. What a novel way to bring the family together.

It gave me that nostalgic thrill to remember the long summers I spent with my mum and her best friend (also a single mother) at Hervey Bay, lying on my stretcher, listening to them complain over a few bottles of Cold Duck.

So our holiday treat for our family of seven was one entire week bunkered down in a sweet little working class van park by the sea. For the generation of kids who view trips to Bali, luxury hotels and the privacy of their own room as an expectation rather than a privilege, regular time in a caravan is the perfect inoculation to protect them from becoming spoilt brats.

I am thinking of promoting a caravan holiday as a brand new form of family therapy. It really brought us together. Literally. There are no fights about clearing the table when you have to sleep on it later that night. Then there's the bliss of a few Facebook, MSN, DVD-free days, where the silence is punctuated only by body gas and other glorious sounds of nature, such as eskies being slammed shut.

Life's Felliniesque sound bites drift by; like the tubby six-year-old in the van next to us who turned to her morbidly obese mum and growled, 'If you're finished with that, can I eat the rest of the chicken?' This sentence punctuated an attempt by my husband and I to make love. It did not help the mood. There's nothing more romantic than trying to slip in a quiet fuck without disturbing the kids in the annex. The old 'don't come a knocking when the van is rocking' was not an anecdote developed without cause. One failed attempt at sex meant we all needed motion sickness tablets.

What I loved most about our holiday at the caravan park was how attractive it made me feel. I'd been having some low self-esteem issues trying to shift my recent baby weight but, as it turned out, by caravan park standards, I was svelte. Hanging my

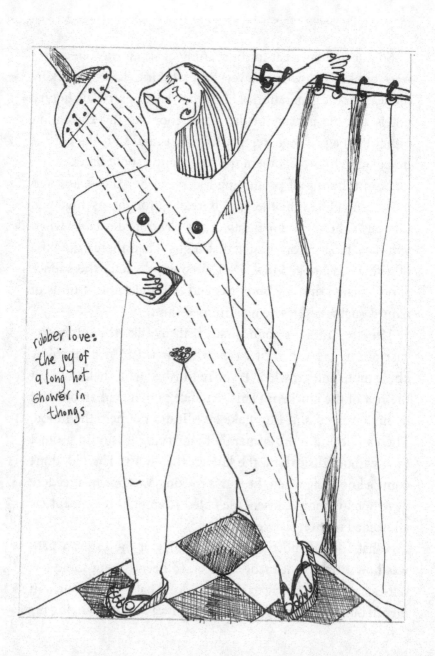

rubber love:
the joy of
a long hot
shower in
thongs

undies on the communal line I noted they were about a quarter of the size of some of the blushing bloomers. Everyone in van parks is so bloody fat. It's amazing watching people emerge from their vans. When you see the size of their girths you can't imagine how they got through the tiny orifice that is the van door. It was like watching a magician pull a pigeon out of his hat. A very, very, very overweight pigeon. I felt like I was at a casting call for *Australia's Biggest Loser: The Caravan Edition.*

During the day we'd swim, or fish, or read and plan the next meal. We abandoned trying to cook in our micro kitchen and lined up at the camp kitchen with all the other sausage schleppers. The kids washed up, they helped set the table, they packed away. Oh bliss! If only we could live in a caravan all the time!

At night we strolled the 'hood, peeking through windows and annexes for a snapshot of people's lives. It's one of my favourite things to do. When I was a child my mother and I used to walk around the neighbourhood and look into people's houses – they always had to be worse off than us – and we'd say, oh, aren't you glad we're not them. Sometimes it was a challenge. It's hard to gloat when you're at the bottom of the food chain.

But doing our nightly van stalking was a hoot. It was better than taking the kids to any art gallery. The van park was like walking right into the frame of a Diane Arbus photograph, 'Elderly pensioners playing cards by candle light', 'Fat man eating fish', 'Ugly child with can of Coke riding tricycle'.

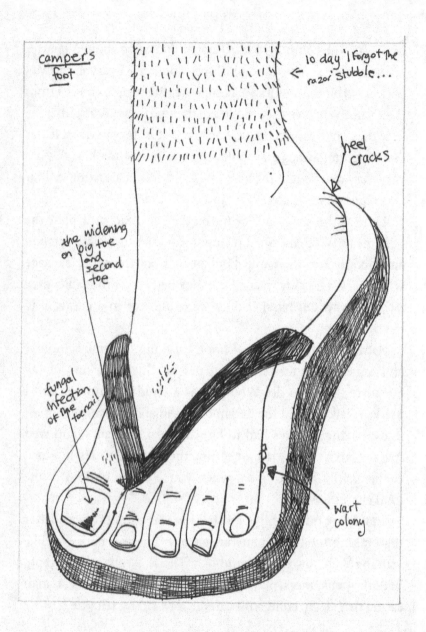

camper's
foot

10 day 'I forgot the
razor' stubble...

heel
cracks

the widening
on big toe
and
second
toe

fungal
infection
of the
toenail

wart
colony

The highlight of our holiday was definitely the family trip to the amenities block and the camaraderie that comes with having only one bar of soap. And one pair of thongs. Somehow, when issuing packing instructions, I forgot the golden rule of van parks: thongs. Walking in thongs, showering in thongs, sleeping in thongs. Caravans parks cannot be negotiated without a pair of double pluggers. It's the rubber passport. The cultural equivalent to travelling abroad and speaking the native tongue. In caravan parks around the country, 'thong' is the first language. Thongs are prophylactics for the feet, protection against plantar warts. Fear of foot warts puts the fear of God into the kids who had forgotten to bring theirs. Instead they opt for showering in their regular shoes.

There's nothing quite as perverse as standing naked under a stream of hot water in your thongs. I'm still not out of the habit. You don't get thong showering at the Versace. No-one fronts up with flip flops at the Hilton. Rubber love is sacred to communal showering and based on the assumption that the poor carry viral infections. There is nothing to say that you couldn't catch plantar warts at a five-star hotel. But they'd be rich warts, and everyone would want them. Plantar prejudice has it pigeonholed for the proletariat. Herpes for the hoi poloi.

While a curse to some, this much maligned wart does have some advantages. On the days we were holed up in the annexe due to inclement weather, the plantar provides hours of fun picking at it with tweezers. There's also something quite magical about the concept that every plantar embedded deep in the foot of every van-dwelling vacationer holds a little DNA of the camper who came before. It is a reminder that, even on the most minute level, as human beings, we are all truly connected through our shared human experience.

For one glorious week, we were hobbits. One wart to bind us ...

# The strap

I do a joke on stage that always gets a huge laugh: when I was a kid, my mother loved using threats. 'You wait till your father gets home,' she'd say and sometimes we'd wait for up to three years. The audience usually gives birth to kittens at this point. It's not really true, though. My father was dead. I think she only said, 'Wait till your father gets home' once. And that was the day he never came back. So it was a pretty major threat. I'd spent all day praying he wouldn't come back. And then he didn't. Turns out, at just six years old, not only could I tie my own shoelaces, I also had the ability to kill people with my thoughts.

I was the last of a generation that got whacked. I have a friend who didn't realise that wooden spoons were used for

cooking until she left home. She found someone stirring some pumpkin soup with a wooden spoon and screamed, 'Get that out of there, that's been on someone's bum!' My friend Jackie experienced discipline via the electric jug cord. This was a long, snaking device with a Bakerlite fitting. It was like being hit with a projectile that could be recoiled and re-aimed. Everything changed for Jackie when her mum came home with a cordless jug. Until she started hitting her with that.

My mum wasn't into using kitchen implements as weapons. Hell, she was flat out using kitchen implements as kitchen implements. Mum did all her best work by hand. Very occasionally my behaviour would push her over the edge and she'd leave a stinging red welt on my arse. It was the perfect behavioural signpost. It was clear that I'd gone too far when I couldn't sit down. I was scared of my mum. I didn't want to get in trouble. I never once told her to get fucked. I wasn't even game to think it. If she asked me to do something I'd do it. I couldn't even imagine what would have happened to me if I'd behaved like my children do with me.

On a recent visit to my nanny I was complaining how hard it was to get the kids to do what they're told. Nanny lifted a heavy arm, the skin flapping like a loose sail as she pointed into the darkest cavern on the back porch. 'You need the strap.' Hanging on a nail in my dead grandfather's grotto was the strap. The family strap. My eyes watered just looking at it. I could feel the pain on a genetic level. My family heritage of struggle and compliance hung limply in the shadows. At the mention of its name, I am sure I saw it quiver. The strap, once an object that inspired fear and obedience, was now just an impotent length of leather. It was the symbol of a dead empire, when children obeyed their parents. The strap had once been powerful. It had wrapped its length around the backs of knees, it had cut the naked flesh of small bums and it had been held above Nanny's head, buckle high, and let fly with a bloodcurdling banshee scream. It was once a violent peacekeeper, but now it was just an old belt. Nanny smiled darkly and narrowed her lashless eyes at me. 'I hit all my kids with that strap, Mandy. I hit your father and I hit you.'

My bum tingled with the memory. I remembered the strap. I only got it once. It was enough. I said, 'We don't hit kids anymore, Nanny. It's against the law.'

'Yeah, and look at kids today,' she humphed. 'There's more of them breaking the law than ever. Give me and the strap one of those kids and we'll have them sorted out quicker than 12 counselling sessions. Only take us 12 seconds.'

Nanny scares me when she talks like that. But she's 94 and blind with a crippled leg. I reckon the average kid's gonna get a head start on her and the strap.

Over time I've discovered that when it comes to disciplining kids, nothing really works. You have to stay one step ahead. Out-think the little buggers. One of my favourite techniques, which I have pioneered myself, is inconsistency. I never react the same way twice. I minimise the big stuff and catastrophise the trivial. For instance, if Charlie failed an exam that he hadn't bothered studying for because he'd spent the last two weeks on his PlayStation I'd say, 'Oh well, good try, love. At least you got to level 6 on your game.' But if he didn't get his lunchbox out of his bag I'd start flapping, 'Bloody hell, what are you thinking? This is a disgrace! An outrage! I'm having you fostered.' Inconsistency puts kids on the back foot. They just can't predict how you are going to respond.

When it comes to making threats, I'm a natural. The secret of a good threat is that the maker should be prepared to carry out no matter how preposterous. Otherwise the child will never learn to trust. Remember when your dad would yell, 'I'm going to beat the living daylights out of you!' And he would. That wasn't child abuse: that was laying the foundations for developing trust.

Sometimes, carrying out the threat can be more challenging than the behaviour it was supposed to modify. Some years back I was having trouble getting four-year-old Charlie into the bath. He was going through that stinky stage where little boys like to dress as Power Rangers or Spiderman. During this phase they refuse to remove the superhero outfit or to bathe. They super reek. My son had been dressed as the Red Ranger for a week. There were urine stains running down the costume's inside leg. The shirt was smeared with vegemite. (God, I hope it was vegemite.) And the pants had a bit of sick on them from our last car trip to the Gold Coast. So I said, 'Get in the bath.'

'No.'

'Charlie, I'm not kidding, get in the bloody bath!'

'No.'

I started to get angry. Now I know that no child has ever died from not bathing, but I didn't want a dirty kid. It makes me look like a shit mum. I want a nice clean kid in funky clothes. I know how we women judge other mothers. If I have to go into public one more time and suffer that roll of the eyes and the mutter under the breath, 'Must be from Nimbin,' I'll go postal. So I issued the threat. 'If you don't get in the bath … I'm going to take you … to … to … to … the cops!' There I said it. My Power Ranger would be brought into line by the cops. Charlie looked at me wide-eyed. 'I mean it.' I don't. 'I will.' I won't. 'You don't believe me?' Clearly he didn't. 'Get in the car!'

Shit! Shit! Shit! I start the car, Red Ranger in the booster. I drive to the cop station. I don't really know how this will go. Neither does Charlie. I hope that he'll lament and agree to the suggested bathing regime before we get there but he doesn't say a word. I pull up outside the cop shop. 'Here we are, Charlie. We are at the police.'

He looks frightened. Maybe even catatonic. He still doesn't believe me. I am a good mother and he needs to see that I am a woman of my word. I march him up to the duty sergeant.

'Right, I can't get him in the frickin' bath … what are you going to do about it?'

The sergeant couldn't get him in the bath either. It just shows you how ineffective our policing has become.

I once used a threat that was so powerful it affected my children's behaviour for years. Children always throw tantrums in supermarkets. It's like they have a secret roster: 'You did it last week, so it's my turn, and then Charlie is rostered for the long weekend.' Any supermarket, anywhere in the world, you'll find a child on its back looking like it's having a grand mall seizure. It's not epilepsy. It's desire. For everything. Have you ever seen a child throw a tantrum in a health food shop? Ever? No. You know why? There's nothing in there they actually want. No self-respecting kid is going to lose it for a dried banana.

Just to preface this story, you need to understand that I send Zoe to a Catholic school. Not because I'm still Catholic, I'm not. I just believe in outsourcing guilt.

I was shopping at Woolies when Zoe was only about eight. She hit the deck. She has a skill level that is awe-inspiring. She was on the tiles flapping like a snapper on the sand. Part of me wanted to mow her down with the trolley. Then this feeling of peace came over me, and a voice that was low and deep and calm emanated from somewhere deep within.

'Zoe, I can see you are having a hard time dealing with your anger right now.' Zoe grew silent. I have never responded like this before. Her eyes were wide. I looked down at her and smiled my sweetest Mummy dearest smile as I cooed, 'So what we're going to do is go to school on Monday and ask them to pray for you at assembly!' She was up and off that floor within seconds. No-one threw a tantrum in my house for years. Religious shaming is a powerful behaviour modifier. You just don't get that at a public school.

I've tried groundings. What a joke. One kid gets grounded and then I have to stay home with them while everyone else goes to the beach. Can't we just leave them in the car? Who's being punished here? Surely a grounding would be more effective if one were to employ old-fashioned 'stocks'. Not outside, that's not sunsafe. I'm talking about on the back patio.

I've tried 'natural consequences'. That's great in theory, but unpredictable in action. 'Sweetie, don't play with the Ratsak. Don't suck the packets ... okay, if you must. Here's a bucket. No, not for the sandpit, it's for when you start vomiting up blood. I don't want stains on the new rug.'

I've set boundaries hundreds of times. I have written a list of rules and regulations as high as the electric fence at Guantanamo Bay and the little shits just dig out underneath. 'You can't have sex until you're 16.' That turns into, 'You can't have sex in my house until you're 16.' Then you come home and find them going at it in the yard. Right on the boundary line.

I've used bribery. Promises of trips to Dreamworld to clean their bedrooms, cash for compliance. I just end up paying my kids to behave. If a man pays a woman for sex he's contracting the loveless services of a hooker. If a mother pays her children to behave, what is she? I know, a frickin' failure!

I try planned ignoring, where I don't react to anything. This is the preferred behaviour management route of Helen Keller but for those of us with all five senses in tact it requires about three valium.

I've tried 'positive reinforcement', using praise and special Mummy time for doing wees in the potty and not punching little brothers in the head. I've even pioneered a few of my own less conventionally approved behaviour modification techniques including 'total abandonment': 'That's it, Mummy's leaving and she's never coming back.' I've used guilt: 'Oh, I think you just gave Mummy cancer.' And there are times when I have just cried. Not tiny girly tears, but large ugly salty sobs. I've sat there and bawled like a baby in sheer and utter despair. This is quite possibly the most effective of all techniques. It's called, 'Mummy's going crazy'. The kids become quiet. They hug me. They say they're sorry. And then they start actually helping. Doing the dishes, cleaning their room, bringing in the washing. I'm just a straight jacket away from a complete nervous collapse, and they're finally loving and respectful. What's a woman got to do to get control of her kids – end up in a mental facility?

Books on behaviour management for terrible toddlers and untameable teens are all well in good if you're living in the fifties with kids who lead the Christian Youth Group. What do you do when your teenage daughter has a meltdown because you won't let her change schools, throws her furniture around the room and then starts screaming abuse at you? The other night I broke the law. When my hysterical daughter was swearing at me, 'I hate you, you fat, fucking whore,' I slapped her across the face. It was like a reflex. And you know what? She backed down. I don't think it was the right thing to do, but I had nothing else.

I couldn't really say, 'If you keep going like that you won't get stickers for your chart! You'll have to stay in your room! No movies on the weekend!' It all seemed a bit lame in the face of out of control verbal abuse.

My daughter apologised. I apologised. We talked softly for an hour. And then I went to bed and crawled up into the foetal position and cried. I felt like a failure. I had no solutions left. No strategies. No new ideas. Only thoughts of violence. John is always excellent in these situations. As I sobbed, 'Pass the phone, I'm going to hand myself into DOCS,' he just laughed and proceeded to give me a foot massage. These are the hardest moments. The moments that tear a couple apart. As a stepfather, John has a remarkable ability to stand behind me in support but doesn't interfere with my parenting. Even when I'm fucking it up. Of course, if required, he'll step in at a moment's notice.

As he massaged my feet he confessed, 'You did really well to control yourself. I stayed away. I would have lost it much worse if she'd gone at me like that.' It's nice of him to make me feel better. But it's not true. He's so much calmer and more rational than me. But that's the act of a good man.

I don't understand why it has become so hard. At no time in history have children been so considered. Although there is still far too many stories of neglect and abuse, I think the average kid has got it pretty good compared to what his or her parents or grandparents lived through. It wasn't that long ago that kids were the 'seen and not heard' half-humans who resided in the shadowy halls of orphanages and boarding schools. These days, kids have opinions. They have passions. They have a sense of self-importance. They not only believe they are equal to their parents; they believe they are right. We've shaped their fragile egos to believe that they're so important and special I wonder how they're going to cope as an adult in a world where they're dismissed as ordinary and inconsequential like the rest of us stupid sheep.

On the whole, most kids have it better than any other generation ever has. They are loved and cherished and indulged. They don't get the strap. They get time to think or sent to the counsellor to work on their issues. Our children have not experienced the high levels of socially approved violence of their predecessors. They haven't been beaten by their parents or their teachers or the cops. But ironically, they are the most violent generation to date. We don't hit them, but they hit us, and each other. I don't endorse violence as a means of behaviour modification. Violence just encourages more violence. But why is it that when we stopped smacking our children that their behaviour spiralled out of control? Is it possible to engender respect without fear?

So I took the strap my nanny offered. It hangs on a nail in the kitchen watching over us. It's like a nuclear weapon. I have no intention of ever using it. Just the sight of it and its legend of fear is deterrent enough. I haven't misbehaved once.

# The big wave

I don't function well in a crisis. I'm a panicker. It's not my fault. It's genetic. I come from a long line of panickers. My mother panicked about everything. She'd get lost negotiating an outer Brisbane suburb and end up a sobbing mess. 'I can't do it,' she'd moan, 'I'll never find the street. Oh, why me? Why is it so hard?'

I was only seven at the time, but even I could see that she was catastrophising. 'It's just Chermside, Mum. I'm sure we won't be eaten by savages.' My mother panicked my entire childhood. Even now if I say, 'Oh no!' she'll give a sharp intake of breath and scream, 'What? What? What's happened?'

I'll say something like, 'Oh, I've put on a kilo.'

My grandmother panicked. And her mother before her. Consequently, my mother never learnt to swim, ride a horse or cross the road independently.

If you want an emotional map that signposts your functionalities and your failures, take note of how you behave in a crisis. Are you the person who makes in the heat of the moment life-changing decisions? Are you the selfless type who puts everyone's needs ahead of their own? Or are you the self-involved dickhead who runs around screaming and putting everyone else's life in danger? I'm the dickhead. In a serious crisis, like a plane crash, it would be best for the safety of all if I was shot first.

I didn't know this about myself until the tsunami. I'm not talking the cataclysmic Indonesian tsunami that claimed well over 300 000 lives. I still find it difficult to comprehend the enormity of that death toll. No, I am talking about the one we had in Australia some six years ago. Or didn't have. The pseudo-nami.

It was the second of April 2007. I'd made it through the morning routine. The children were all at school. I was at the offices of *The Echo*, a small town newspaper where I write a weekly opinion piece and edit the entertainment pages. I was at the photocopier. One of the journalists dropped her laptop bag on the desk and grins. 'Have you heard about the tsunami warning?'

Yesterday was April Fool's Day. I'm a comedian. You can't get me that easily. 'Yeah, good one. Check the calendar, April Fool's was yesterday.'

My colleague was suddenly serious. 'No, it's real. There's been an alert put out for the whole east coast of Australia. I've been on the beach taking photos.'

*Jesus. She's serious.* I gulp. 'When?'

'They expect the wave to hit in about an hour and a half.' She plonked down on her chair and started booting up her computer. I addressed the receptionist and the sales assistant in what I hoped was an offhand and nonchalant manner. Panickers don't like to be exposed as neurotics amongst their peers. 'Is this true?' They all nodded casually. Apparently tsunami warnings don't mean much at a country newspaper. Still got to sell ads. Ten metres of wave coming your way is the perfect opportunity to sell full page ads to surf shops.

'So what about the schools?' My colleague began downloading her photos.

'Oh, they haven't given them evacuation orders yet but they have instructed them to be ready.'

Wow. At that time I had three kids at three different schools. I contemplated downsizing the family by just picking up one. I'd pick up Sophia, the middle child. She'd never expect it.

Now I was starting to panic. My hands were sweating. My heart was racing. I imagined a huge wave sweeping through Byron Bay and not being able to get my children. It made me feel nauseous. I was embarrassed by my reaction. Everyone else in the office looked so calm. I began to leave, making my excuses. 'Forgot I had to drop the car off for a service.'

I sprinted to the car park. There was just over an hour before T-Time. I had to get to Zoe's high school in Lennox Heads. *Oh God, it's beachfront.* That was a 20-minute drive, then I had to get Charlie from his alternative school and Sophia from the Catholics, then I had to find the highest, safest point and park. As I am trying to make this plan I reversed right into someone's car.

It was a BMW. Of course it was. I broke the front headlight and dented the bonnet a bit. Is it really necessary to leave your contact details if the end of the world is nigh? I haven't checked my comprehensive insurance lately but I don't think it covers this impending apocalypse. I was halfway out of the car park when guilt gets the better of me. Bloody hell. I run back with a business card and popped it under the windshield.

I decided to pick up the two closest kids first. I arrived at Charlie's alternative school. Fortunately, the majority of the alternative parents were as paranoid as me, so most of the kids have been cleared out. The only kids who hadn't been picked up were the ones whose parents were too stoned to drive.

Charlie was only in kindergarten and had no idea why I was picking him up. I mumbled something about a big wave coming and he looked disinterested as we cross the road to get Sophia. 'Does Chookie have to come too?' he inquired, using Sophia's pet name.

'Yes, we are all going.'

'Why?' I'm embarrassed. What do you say to a six-year-old boy without giving him an anxiety attack? But then he should know what's going on. I'm not one of those parents who believes in lying to your children to protect them. I decided a plain English approach would be best.

'Well, there's a huge wave coming that will drown everyone in this town.' He immediately started to cry.

'Will I die?'

'No darling, that's why Mummy's taking you somewhere safe.' He was white-knuckled with terror and held my hand so tightly the end of my fingers turned purple.

I had to sign Sophia out. Bloody protocol. I was clearly not abducting her. There's an impending tsunami and I had to wait in the office for the appropriate note to be signed so my child can be released. Great. We were losing valuable time. This delay could end up leaving us in a low lying area. Oh well, at least we would die with all our paperwork in place.

When I finally presented the yellow note to the teacher I was rewarded with my daughter, wide-eyed with excitement. She was being picked up. She was one of the chosen ones. There is nothing sadder than the faces of the children who aren't being picked up. They were terror stricken. I tried not to look at them. 'Don't worry kids,' I shouted as I ran from the classroom, 'just grab your desks and kick!'

Charlie and Sophia began laughing as we jumped in the car and hit the road. 'What about Daddy?'

*Shit. I hadn't even rung him.* In my maternal frenzy I'd made plans to rescue my babies, but I'd totally forgotten to rescue Russ. I suppose I should have realised then that my heart wasn't in the marriage. Forty minutes til wave time and my husband was at work without a car below sea level. I was leaving the poor bugger to drown.

'Daddy wasn't answering his phone, I'll try him again,' I lied. I sped towards Lennox Head to collect Zoe. Russ answered his phone. I gave him the lowdown. He was completely aware of the whole tsunami situation and was unimpressed. I was running out of time, but I offered to pick him up. He laughed and said brusquely, 'Forget it, I've got a class. I've got too much work to do.' *Great. I don't have to pick him up. We may make it after all.*

Zoe was only too delighted to be escorted from her tartan prison. As soon as we hit the car she kicked off her shoes and socks, unbuttoned her shirt and let out her hair. 'I'm hungry,' she demanded.

I didn't really know where we were heading. I had the news on and the tsunami updates kept flooding through. It was only 25 minutes until they expected the wave to hit the east coast of Australia. I wanted to be sick. I took the back roads that wound towards a spectacular roadside lookout. I couldn't think of anywhere else. People might die, but at least we would have a good view.

I thought we'd be the only ones. I pulled up with just minutes to go and had to fight for a park. There are only three or four spaces at the best of times and that day there were around 50 people at the lookout, just standing there watching the horizon, where a bright blue strip of ocean met the land.

I noted with some suspicion two SES guys in their orange shirts, squatting down having a cup of tea. I thought they were supposed to be at ground zero. Bloody cowards.

The kids and I joined the small crowd of fellow neurotics. In an awful moment of self realisation I was struck with the revelation that we all mentally unwell. We, the anxiety prone, huddled together to watch the rest of the functional world drown in the wake of a massive wall of water.

Nothing happened. The wave hit time came and went and not one of us noticed a thing. My eyes were hurting from staring so hard into the distance. The kids were unimpressed. Their fear and excitement melted into boredom. What started out as a natural disaster has ended in a big long wait for nothing. Like most of their small lives, great expectation was met with disappointment. In that regard, I'm nothing if not consistent.

We, the neurotic, gathered in our sombre silence, actually wanting the wave to come. We couldn't get off our hill for the shame of being wrong, and the fear of returning to our homes and our work places to be branded 'fucking idiots'. No-one was really talking. One of the blokes had his car door open and the ABC news updates were blaring.

The kids were starting to complain. I couldn't stand it. 'I'm going.'

There's shock from the mob. Then the unofficial mob leader, the bloke with the radio, stood up to block my way to the car. He said, 'I wouldn't go yet. It hasn't been called off!'

Called off? You don't call off a natural disaster. 'Today in Australia we had to call off the tsunami due to lack of interest.

Only one per cent of the population were willing to respond. They are now on medication.'

So I stayed a little longer. Zoe was sitting in the car texting her friends. Charlie was enjoying the free time and rolling in the long grass on the side of the lookout. It's very tense in the crowd. No one speaks for at least five minutes. Then Sophia pipes up.

'I shave my pubes.'

*What?* 'What did you just say?'

'I shave my pubes.' It was so random that I couldn't quite comprehend the sense of what she'd just said. Her words hung in the silence. Strange looks of accusation floated my way. Other people shielded their children and moved them away from the strange shaving family.

'I don't.' I blurt out, 'and she doesn't either, she's only eight!'

I glared at Sophia, furious that she had embarrassed me. She pointed wordlessly at the roof of the makeshift shelter at the lookout. In tiny pencil writing someone had graffitied, 'I shave my pubes.'

I started laughing. But not just a little giggle. I was hysterical. I was coughing, spluttering 'I shave my pubes' and pointing. The crowd thought I had gone nuts. I tried to justify myself. 'It's written … someone did it … and then drove here … and wrote it.' I was crying with laughter imagining some man or woman with a prickling pubis so compelled by their hairless genitalia that they felt the compulsion to share it with the world via pencil scribble on a random lookout.

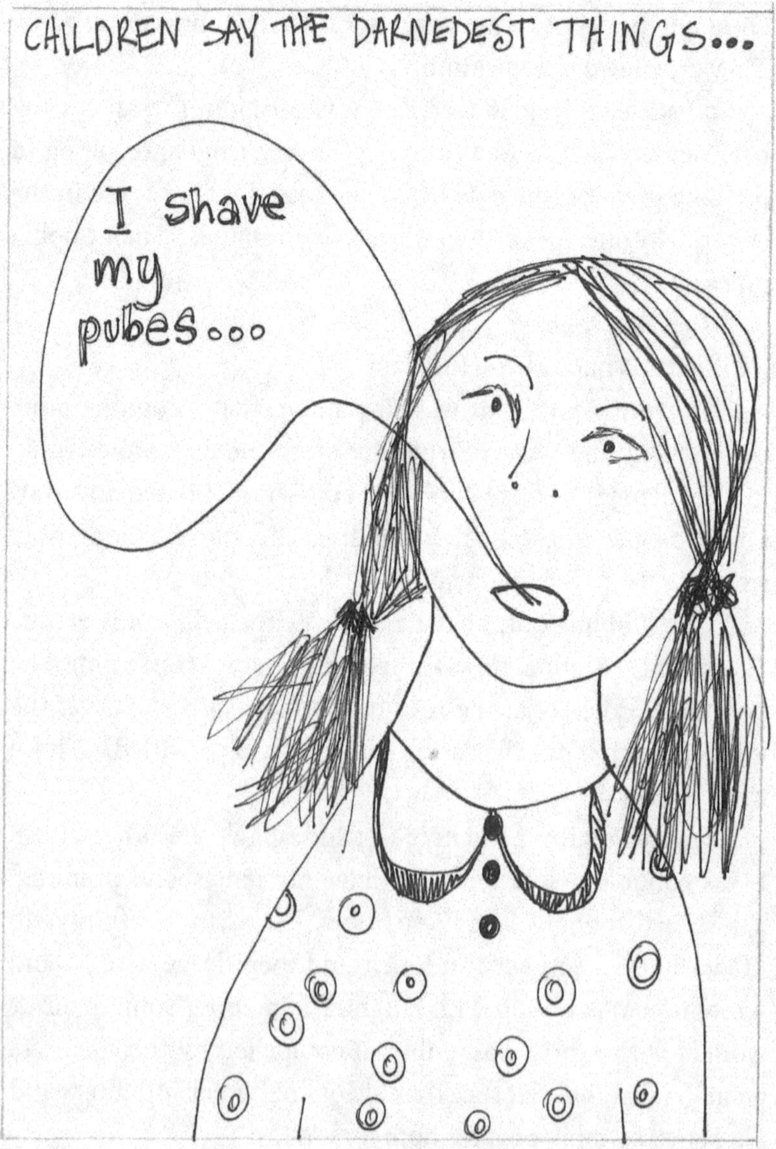
CHILDREN SAY THE DARNEDEST THINGS...
I shave my pubes...

I decided to leave. 'Get in the car.' The kids were relieved. I promised them the rest of the day off school. They thought I was being nice, but the truth was I was too embarrassed to drive them back.

We were heading towards home when I noticed Zoe scratching her crotch. 'Are you itchy, sweetie?' I'm a good mum of daughters so I'm always on thrush alert.

'Yeah, a bit … I shaved my pubes.'

Oh my God. What the hell did I do to make that happen?

# Everything you've ever wanted to know about sex (genital warts and all)

What I would do if I were you:
Lie

Every parent dreads the 'sex' talk. Even the most liberal of us blushes when forced to ruin a six-year-old's innocence with 'and then the daddy puts his penis in the mummy's vagina.' There's just no nice way of delivering the news. Suddenly the child who believes fairies exchange teeth for money like a dental version of cash converters or that a giant beatific rabbit delivers chocolate eggs is being hit with life's most surreal and pornographic reality. Penises go into vaginas. Like a Lego man stuck to his block. Like a plug goes into a socket or a plastic card goes into an auto teller: we fit together.

Sex is weird. The means of human reproduction is more like fantasy than actual fantasy. It's hard to get your head around the fact that residing in the hairy balls of some bloke at the pub is one half of the next potential prime minister. Santa's sack is mythical, the bloke's at the pub is magical. Who would have guessed? I still know who I'd rather have come down my chimney.

Zoe nearly wet herself when I delivered the 'sex' talk. She couldn't stop laughing. At every turn she shrieked, 'No, you're making it up!' Then I started laughing so much I couldn't breathe. When you try and describe it, sex is absolutely ridiculous. Explaining how babies are made is a lot harder than telling someone how to make a pancake. I'd rather describe breaking an egg than fertilising one.

When I tell Zoe that the man moves his penis around and this special substance comes out the end and travels up the tube inside the woman's vagina all the way to the egg, she screamed, 'No, no, that's just silly!' She didn't believe me! I'm the same woman who told her about fairies and the Easter Bunny. There's obviously a giant chasm between the dual realities of biology and fantasy. Maybe I should have told her that babies were something you downloaded from the internet or photocopied, or were moths that found their way into your undies and took up residence in the uterus. In the end I wimped out. We all wimp out. No-one really tells their kids about sex. We tell them how babies are formed. We tell them how babies grow. And then, as if hoping they'll never ever have sex themselves, we tell our poor daughters how babies get out. It's graphic. It's disturbing. Anyone who's got a vagina and hears a story like that is not going to sleep for a week. Maybe not ever. If we were to be culturally accurate with our procreative sex talk then we should also give the kids a run down on gay and lesbian couples who use donor sperm, IVF procedures for infertile couples and then the naughty mummies who get pregnant and have a baby without the daddy really ever knowing.

Our children's introduction to sex initially is that it's purely a biological process. Something akin to doing a poo or having a tooth pulled, a vaguely unpleasant and uncomfortable experience but it must be endured to achieve the end result. No-one tells their kids that human beings generally have sex for pleasure. No-one says, 'Well your mummy's a bit of a slut.' No, mummies and daddies perform this bizarre penis and vagina act solely to have babies, and that's why Mummy takes this special pill every morning. It's a baby enhancer. No-one tells their kids about orgasm. Or masturbation. Or fellatio. Or faking it. There's no book on the shelf that really helps you explain to your kids how freaking amazing sex is even when it's ordinary, and that sometimes, if you're not careful, you'll end up making a baby, and then the mummy will get stuck with that daddy for a while, until she can find a more suitable one.

Well, that's what this mummy did. Talking to my kids about sex I felt like such a fraud pretending I'd only ever had sex with their dads. Sure, I've got three times as many dad notches than most mums have on their bedposts but it was still a big dirty lie. I am an advocate for honesty with children, but how do you tell your kids, 'Sex is wonderful. It's natural. And before Mummy met Daddy, she had over 50 partners. And yes, she did make a few babies early on, but she had abortions.' Now that makes pretty meaty news for any kindergarten kid.

As a woman, I believe it's my moral obligation to prepare my four daughters for a world where they are in control of their own sexuality. That means they need to know their own bodies. They need to be able to speak about sexuality, about pleasure and about their bodies without embarrassment or shame. These are girls who are going to grow up being able to have sex with the lights on. As a woman who's spent most of her life fumbling in the dark with a high libido and low self-esteem, I believe that it's one of the greatest gifts I can impart. As for my son, growing up around empowered women, I don't have to tell him a thing. Ten minutes at the dinner table with his insouciant sisters and he's au fait with genital piercing, labioplasty and premature ejaculation. At age nine he has more information about sex than he's ever going to need. Every time he gets emotional or throws a mini-tantrum about his exile from the bathroom one of the girls unkindly quips, 'Charlie's got his period!'

As three of my daughters are all in the pubescent blush, Lolita-like and lethal, I decided it was time for the most confronting talk of all. The REAL sex talk. I told them everything. Well, everything I knew. It took over a week. There's just so much subject area. We talked about orgasm. About masturbation. About enjoying their bodies. I was so embarrassed talking about this I was almost ill. I've never seen them pay so much attention. Facebook was shut down

my children give me the sex talk...

and phones were turned off. Wide-eyed they sat on the couch, clutching cushions, desperate to get as much information as they could. We talked about ovulation, about menstrual cycles, about how periods synch up; we talked about cunninglingus, about fellatio, about vibrators, about girls giving boys wristies at school, what vaginas look like, about why women have more energy after sex and men have none. We talked about anal sex. (The girls decided to give that a big miss. The prude in me was relieved. I don't know much about anal. I talked about contraception, and about the side effects. I told them that unfortunately most contraception makes you fat. And ironically, not using contraception makes you fat as well. It was decided rather unanimously that condoms were preferable.

We talked about erections, scrotums and how boys don't always like using condoms. We talked about girls having sex with girls, boys having sex with boys and girls having sex with two boys or two girls having sex with one boy. We talked about saying no to sex, about dealing with unwanted sexual advances, about 40-year-old men with a penchant for young things who'll always give it a crack. We talked about female ejaculation, about being frigid, about herpes and genital warts and the mind-warping effects of syphilis.

Man, you need a degree in sex education to do this kind of talk. When I started the conversation I suddenly realised that I don't know that much. Like how many days a month do you ovulate? Three I think? Although I was tempted to tell them 20 just to be on the safe side. Are the G spot and clitoris connected? I don't really know. Possibly. Let's just say that the clit is the warm up act and the G spot is the main act. A lot of people leave at half time, but still enjoy the show.

Then we talked about love. About having your heart broken. About surrendering yourself to a man and baring your soul, and then being rejected. About crawling up into the foetal position and sobbing into the carpet. How do you prepare a girl for having her heart used as an emotional dartboard by the insensitive pricks she'll choose as boyfriends? My girlfriend tells a story of her first heartbreak. She was curled in the hallway bawling like a baby when her mother came inside with some groceries. She stepped over the top of her and snapped, 'For God's sake, get off the floor and go and get the rest of the shopping out of the car.' Now that's good mothering. A girl's gotta get on with it.

After the talk was over I felt as though I'd done my job. I had a smug sense of feminist righteousness, like I'd overcome my own sexual repression and educated my daughters into their own sexuality. I'd opened the door. Information would make them safe. They'll tell me everything. They can trust me. I am so much cooler than my mum. I've really set them up. Good on me. Two days later I opened the door to the bathroom and walked in on my 15-year-old daughter in the shower. (We do this all the time, there's seven of us in a house with one bathroom. I know, it's unbelievable, and possibly contravenes the human rights charter, but as long as one of you is prepared to take the occasional piss in the yard, it works just fine. And hey, it's good for the environment. The lemon tree is awesome.)

not tonight dear
... the sex
talk gave me
a headache...

Anyway, I'd recently installed a see-through shower curtain and on that particular day I got an eyefull. Zoe had given herself a full brazilian. I freaked out. Cool mum, Ms I'm-so-right-on-with-your-sexuality lost the plot.

'You've only just grown pubes, and now you're shaving them off? Are you making porn on the weekends or something?'

My daughter rolled her eyes and grabbed the towel. 'Geez, you're a perve. Everyone does it. Rachel's been doing it for ages.'

I freaked out again. 'But she's just 14!'

'Mum, all the kids call you "Bushie" and stuff if you don't do it.'

Really, like who's looking at your pubic mound at school? 'Good morning class, have you done your homework, and show us your map of Tassie.' At what point in the sex talk was I supposed to tell them not to shave their pubic hair off? A full brazilian is a lover's special treat, a pre-requisite for risqué lingerie shoots and surgery preparation for tubal ligation. It's not something teenage girls should be doing as a matter of course. I'm surprised they can even walk to the bus stop. The itching must be unbearable. Ironically though, with all that shaving, in ten years' time their pubic area is going to look like Barry White's fro. Man, am I going to laugh. Until then, I've confiscated all the razors. If they want a full brazilian then they can wax. I may not be very good at being a cool mum, but I'm a natural at cruel mum!

# Sleep with me

I haven't had a full night sleep now since 1995. I've been a mother for 15 years so I'm used to the whole 'death of self' concept. I've been dead now for over a decade. I thought at 42 after having a trillion kids I'd be such a pro at mothering that if there was ever an Insomnia Olympics I'd be a contender.

'Nolan approaches the bed. She's still wearing her makeup and jeans. She falls, no, collapses, onto the bed. She's tossing. Nice form on the steal-the-doona roll. What's this? She's dropped off to sleep. There's the baby scream. She's up. Nice save. This is the fifth consecutive night. One more and it's gold for Australia. Uh oh, she's just driven a fork into her eye.'

I don't fantasise about being molested by George Clooney while bent over the dishwasher (maybe the washing machine) or being fondled by Johnny Depp while hosing out the compost bucket (well, just this one time). I fantasise about sleep. This is the ultimate mother erotica:

*'Mandy lay naked between the crisp white sheets. Her breath caused her breast to undulate up and down, up and down, up and down. All night long. It is now 8 a.m. and she's still not up. '*

It's pornographic.

I drive past those signs on the highway that read, 'Do you want longer lasting sex?' Are you kidding me? The ad company creative who created those slogans had to be a bloke under the age of 22. Middle-aged women don't want longer lasting sex. They want nice short sex. Two hours bad. Two minutes good. I can't be having sex for hours at a time. I have a life to lead. Washing to fold. TV to watch. I was so impassioned by the last ad I came across that I snuck back in the dead of night to graffiti it with, 'Do you want longer lasting sleep?' Apparently so many women phoned in that it shut down the switchboard.

Single childless people sleep. I can see it on their faces. I hate them for it. Them and their pillow-creased cheeks and their stupid bed hair. I hate how rested they look. People with kids live in a perpetual state of fatigue. That's why we let our kids loose in the supermarket. It's our only revenge.

Having a baby really hurts. That's an understatement. It's pretty well the equivalent of having a limb removed without anaesthetic, or having to pay a credit card bill long after the squillions of meaningless incidental purchases have bitten the dust. Despite this I'm not a believer in pain relief during labour. Pain is a necessary evil. It's nature's initiation into your life as a parent where intense joy constantly mingles with intense discomfort.

Lesson one in becoming a parent: you need to accept the fact that you may never sleep again. Your sleep is dependent on your children's sleep. I thought that babies were born knowing how to sleep. I thought sleeping was like eating or shitting. It's something that's innate. You eat, you shit, you sleep. Apparently not. Babies need to be taught to sleep. They need to be swaddled tighter than a dim sim and left half-cooked in the cot. The parent is to ignore the cries. The cries are part of the 'self-settling'. Then they start screaming. Sobbing. Sometimes they will yell out, 'Mumma, mumma' in the most heart-wrenching wail. Some of them will beat their heads on the rail of the cot and others will vomit. You aren't supposed to buckle. You are supposed to have your cup of tea and finish the crossword. This is called controlled crying. It's where the parent is encouraged to ignore the call of their infant so they learn to separate and self-soothe. They also learn a few other important life lessons, like when you're scared or traumatised, don't bother asking for help because no-one will come. Imagine trialling the controlled-crying technique on your closest girlfriend, who's just been dumped by her boyfriend. When she rings in tears sobbing, 'I'm so heartbroken … I just want to die …' CLICK. 'Hello, is anyone there?' Sorry Marjorie, but it's for your own good.

I can't do controlled crying. I never could. With all four of my babies, I made myself available to them at every moment. Consequently, none of them has ever really learnt to sleep. With my son, Charlie, we'd sit up and wait for him to collapse from exhaustion. He'd get so hyperactive from lack of sleep he'd sprint around the lounge room. Russ and I would sit on the couch like zombies watching him leaping off the dining table or swinging from the curtains. Eventually he'd trip over or hit his head and we'd say, 'Great, bedtime!' Not because he actually fell asleep, but because he was unconscious. He slept with us until he was seven. Looking back I suspect that was part of the reason why our relationship failed. A child in the bed is the best contraceptive. It's the ultimate barrier method.

When John and I had Ivy I swore that I wouldn't let that happen again. While I absolutely adore having my baby in the bed with us, I didn't want our relationship to be dominated by a kid who refused to sleep in their own room.

But Ivy certainly had other ideas and proved herself to be quite the strategist when it came to conjuring up ways to keep herself in the big bed.

Every night we put our baby girl to sleep in her cot and one hour later she would wake up. That was it. That was the sum total of 'me' time that my precious bundle allocated. In that hour I spent quality time with the four other kids, I answered my emails, did the odd painting, make love to my partner and cleaned the house. It was a pretty massive hour.

I don't think I've managed to have an uninterrupted thought in years, let alone a poo. I hate hearing women complain about their babies waking in the night. I think, waking at three in the morning? Half your luck, that means they've already slept for nine straight hours you unappreciative bitch! I'd be weeping with joy!

I may look like a nice straight mum with a freshly ironed shirt and beige slacks, but at heart, I'm a filthy dirty co-sleeper. I've got a cot but it's just there for show, so when my friends come around they don't know my terrible secret: that I can't teach my children to sleep. The cot is all white and perfect. It's flounced up like a fluffy cloud. To the unwitting visitor, the baby's room is a vision of nouveau nursery perfection. Handmade dollies nestle against felted lambs, soft woollen blankies are folded on the dresser and the night duckie puts out a soft yellow glow. But basically, the baby only goes in there for nappy changes. She's in bed with us. I think it's genetic. My mother confessed that she used to sleep with me. I didn't get my own room until I was 16.

Ivy breastfeeds from about 10 p.m. until 6 a.m. Non-stop. She feeds so heavily she has little need for food and nutrition during the day. I wake up feeling like one of those poppers that's had all the juice sucked out. I can't say no. She loves her night titty. And who wouldn't? It's a delicious bond. Just her and I cuddled up in the corner, a mummy sow and her suckling pig.

I don't separate from my children well. I lie there listening to them breathe, and when they go quiet I poke them to make sure

they're not dead. So I decided to ring a sleep nazi. A woman who comes to your home and for $600 she does what I should have been able to do – teach my child to sleep. My partner is also hoping that for $600 she'll provide some of the wifely services that I've been neglecting since the baby turned up.

Paying someone to teach your baby to sleep is like taking out an ad that says, 'I am a failure as a mother.' If I was the mother of just one kid then I could justify my poor technique. I watch teen mums belting their kids at K-mart and think, *Geez, I bet they get their kids to sleep.* Just to escape the awful reality they have to wake to each day. I might look like some giant Viking queen but I just can't do tough love. Every time I've attempted stupid controlled crying, *I've* ended up crying, uncontrollably.

It just seems so unfair. Why should little babies be forced to sleep alone when we get to snuggle up with a partner? So Ivy is the centrepiece of our marital bed. Amazingly, the tiny body, just 80 cm long, has the capacity to occupy at least half of the king-size bed. She has developed a Ninja-like wall pinning technique that positions me on the mattress perimeter to enable her to stretch out and enjoy that brand new king-size $2000 cushioned comfort. The life force is strong in this one.

Of all my children I would say that Ivy is the most intense, the most energetic and the most inflexible. I named her after my 94-year-old crotchety old nanny, and that's exactly what I got. An adorable tyrant made entirely of breast milk and will. And so that will must be broken.

Sleep nazi turned out to be a pretty young Irish girl. My husband was impressed. I've never seen him so interested in finding out about sleeping routines. He was sitting up at the kitchen table, with the pamphlets spread out nodding attentively, asking all the right questions. Irish sleep nazi says, 'I'm just going to follow you around and watch your routines.'

John couldn't help himself and pipes up. 'After dinner we all have a bath together. You can join us if you like.' Sleep nazi goes very quiet and wide-eyed. I sense she wants to leave but she joins us in the bath anyway. That's good follow through!

As I'm the breastfeeding mother it's decided that John should do all the settling because having me trying to get Ivy back to sleep is the equivalent of teasing an obese person with a Mars Bar. Excellent. The first night Ivy wakes 17 times. Poor John looked as though he'd been backed over by a truck. Sitting up at three in the morning singing, 'Baa Baa Black Sheep' while patting a restless bubba is not the leisure choice of most 50-year-old men. That will teach him for hooking up with a younger woman. While it's terribly upsetting to hear her call for me and not be able to respond, the comfort of the doona and the joy of an unmunched breast gives me some respite.

The next night we were supposed to do the Cry Down – 20 minutes of leaving the baby to cry, hoping that she'd be so exhausted and despondent that she'd just give up and pass out. The first night we did it and it was hell. John and I sat on the couch listening to Ivy scream. First the angry cry. Then the sad

I think my husband is sleeping around...

cry. Then the pleading cry. The cry that said, 'Why don't you love me?' I looked over at John. He was weeping.

'Lets not do this,' I say. 'Let's just go in and pat her. Leave her in the cot and just pat her. It's not like we'll be doing it when she's 18.'

So we disobeyed our sleep trainer. We didn't move to Phase Two. When she phoned for the update we lied. We said, 'Oh yes, it went really well. She's sleeping ... like a baby.' We paid $600 and lied to the sleep trainer. But Ivy is out of the bed. And so is John. He's in the baby's room patting her off. He's okay. Sleeping on the floor has proved therapeutic for his back.

But the real good news is: I'm finally sleeping through.

# On weight

Every day I wake up and think, *Christ, where have I gone?*
Ironically, the less there is of me in my life, the more of me there
actually is. It's my pattern. The busier I get with the kids, the
more of my self I pour into my family, the chubbier I get. Just
the other day when I mounted the scales I swear they groaned.
The digital screen flashed, the numbers whirled: 90.3 kilos
Excellent. I am now 5 kilos heavier than I was at 40 weeks
pregnant with Ivy.

One day I was in my bedroom fighting my way into a pair of
beige control top undies and moaning, 'Oh my God, I'm soooo
fat.' My husband, who was reading, peered professor-like over
his glasses and smiled as he looked at me with a soft beatific

gaze that said, 'I think you're beautiful.' But he said nothing. Surely he must be wondering what happened to that sexy blonde goddess he fell in love with. God knows I am. He went back to his book.

'How can you stand me?' I said somewhat frantically. 'I don't even know how you can bear sleeping in the same bed as me, I'm like a frickin' walrus. Honestly, have you ever seen me this fat?' These are the conversations that frighten men. There is nowhere to go. There is no 'right' answer. It's the relationship equivalent of standing on a landmine. At some point you are going to have to lift your foot and when that happens, you are history, baby.

John murmered, 'You're still breastfeeding, and you haven't been able to exercise ...' He's so sweet. I feel like punching him in the head. Instead I burst into tears. There is no consolation that even touches the sides for a woman who feels fat. Except chocolate. I find myself crying in the fridge, seeking the comfort of peppermint Lindt balls. They're the only balls who know how to say the right thing every time.

There's a 'mother' look. We've all seen it. A flattening of the arse, a rounding and bloating of the gut, a sagging engorgement of the breasts (with the right support you can now create the matronly 'bosom' – a giant beanbag mono-style breast where family members may gain comfort), the loose flapping upper arm sported by all good tuckshop ladies, the red raw chaffed thighs replete with hail damage surface veins, and extra chin flesh that hangs from the neck like a pelican beak. On a good day a close-up of my varicose veins looks like a section of Google maps. Just one husband ago, I'd fought my way back from early onset of flabby middle age. I'd given up booze, I'd gone high protein and I started exercising. Every day. I became one of the women I hate. I was a 'hot mum'.

I dropped 20 kilos and developed a chronic self-esteem problem. I thought I was a lot better than I actually was. I couldn't love myself enough. I bought skimpy bikinis, I dressed in skinny jeans with tight T-shirts. I wore micro-minis and platform shoes. I even started wearing those slutty little Daisy Duke denim shorts. I ironed my hair, I got false nails and a spray tan. I did a TV ad campaign for a beauty therapist promoting permanent hair removal and cellulite treatments, in exchange for … cellulite treatments. I had my broken capillaries zapped and my nasal hair waxed. I was even considering anal bleaching. I had gone from being a mumsy slob to a high maintenance woman. The kind you see at pick-up time and think, *Jesus does that woman have nothing else to do except body renno's*? I started looking at fat mums with a critical tut tut of, 'How could you let yourself go like that. Lazy bitch.' I was smug. As the kilos fell away, so did my compassion. I was so up myself I didn't need a vibrator. And life got me back. I met the man of my dreams (third and final attempt), had a baby girl, the last of my litter at 41 and I got fat again. God piled on the karmic kilos.

Now I'm the lazy, fat bitch sitting in the playground in sensible shoes and bike pants. I'm not wearing bike pants because I'm a closet triathlete. No, it stops my thighs from chaffing. I'm constantly in search for the perfect pair of undies. When you're overweight they tend to roll down or create a side cleavage. I can't wear those restrictive undies, the ones they call Control Tops. They make my kidneys hurt. I can't work out how they are supposed to be slimming when you get this giant fat bubble out the top.

When I look at the drawer that contains my knickers there is not one comfortable pair in there. They've all got the tortured appearance of most of my clothing. You see, I'm stubborn. I won't up-size. I insist on wearing my usual 12–14 when in reality I'm a 16–18. My buttons pop. Zips strain to contain all that woman. If I decide to sit down suddenly there's a chance I'm going to give my self an unintentional tubal ligation. I don't mind being a little voluptuous. I'll strap on an apron, bend over a mixer and purr all Nigella like, but in reality I want to be a sylph. I want to be the mum in a tight denim skirt with a slutty T-shirt. Of course, I still wear those clothes; I just look like I've walked off the set of *Kath and Kim*. I used to think, *Oh well, at least I'm not as fat as Sharon*. Then I picked up a *Women's Weekly*. That Magda's such a bitch. She's not supposed to lose weight. Didn't she realise that she was the fat girl that made us all feel good about ourselves? She's supposed to *stay* fat.

Now even Magda's hotter than me. Oh God, I've run out of Lindt balls.

This isn't the first time I've gotten fat. When I was pregnant with Charlie I gained 30 kilos. One day one of my platform thongs actually exploded under the pressure. He was a whopping

11 pounds (5 kilos). It was like giving birth to a fish. Everyone at the birth centre had to come and see the 'big baby'.

At the time we were living in Sydney. When Charlie was about six weeks old, I gained enough milk-soaked confidence to attempt a Bondi shopping trip and the day seemed totally perfect when I located this really cute little T-shirt. It read, 'I love Charlie.' I thought, now that is perfect! The biggest they had was a size 12, so I bought it as an 'incentive' item for my planned post-baby body war. But I loved it so much I had to wear it straight away. So I wore it to the P and C meeting I had at my daughter Zoe's school. She was in kindergarten, and like many aspirant first-time parents the intention to be the most incredible, involved parent in the world still shone bright. It was the only school committee meeting I have ever attended.

We lived in Greenwich, a very conservative North Shore suburb, where at 42 you were considered to be a 'young mum'. So at 33 with three kids, I was a child bride. I didn't know anyone. Children provide the ultimate opportunity for adults to make friends without anyone actually realising that you are some poor sad friendless loser. So I decided to wear the shirt as an ice breaker. *So what if I have a roll of tummy exposed between my hipsters and the bottom of my shirt,* I told myself. *I've just had a baby. It's mummy fat.*

No-one talked to me at the meeting. In a sea of corporate mothers in Italian suits and balding fathers with cable knit jumpers I was like someone who'd got lost on her way to the caravan park showers. The only time anyone even looked in my direction was when I moved in my chair and the squeak of plastic sounded like I farted. I'm sure everyone thought I did. It's not like you can defend yourself.

I felt humiliated by my failure to engage anyone in a conversation or say anything remotely meaningful. I was so upset. I arrived home in tears and told Russ the story. He motioned towards my shirt. 'Did you wear that?'

I'm always sensitive to Russ's comments about my weight because his dad was a very vocal fatty hater, and Russ himself admitted when pressed that he didn't find me attractive when I was overweight. I was about to initiate a feminist argument on post-baby bodies and how women needed time to settle into motherhood when he interrupted. 'You wore a shirt that says, "I love Charlie" to a school meeting?'

I nodded. 'I thought it was cute.'

He started to laugh. 'Mandy, don't you know what that means?' I stared at him blankly.

'This is Sydney. It means I love cocaine.' Shit. I wore a druggie shirt to the P and C meeting. Now everyone at my daughter's straight-laced little school thought I was a drug slut. In the year that I was there, I made friends with only two women, one of them was a pot dealer and the other one was on the methadone program.

Losing weight is never easy. I have always loved bad men and carbs. I've sorted out the bloke situation and now I need to wave goodbye to my carbs as well. It's so sad. I adore crunchy white bread. I become aroused when confronted with the soft

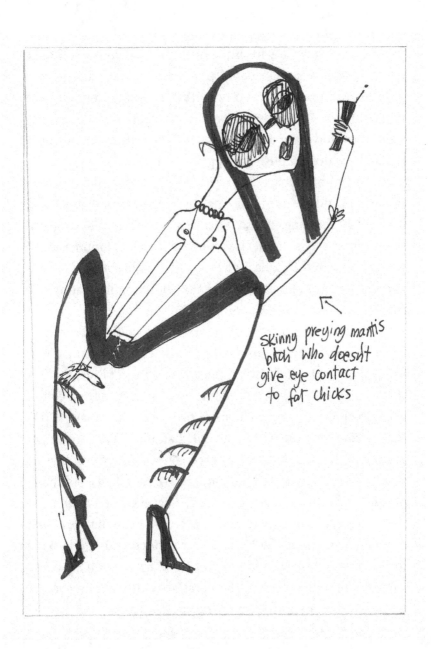

powdered pastry of a freshly made almond croissant. I once fell in love with a man based purely on the fact that he had his own pasta machine. But now it's back to high protein. But there's only so much meat a woman can take. When I get pre-menstrual and have a hissy fit, what do I do now? Fry up a steak? How do you push down pain with meat?

It's not comfortable being overweight. Everything hurts. I go to the pool and the most I can manage is three laps. It's not being overweight that bugs me so much, it's the inherent lethargy. I'd really rather stay at home, watch telly and eat. Fat mums spend more time with their kids. It's a fact. They might live shorter lives and make their kids fatter by role modelling comfort eating, but they're always at home. Cooking. Eating. Crying.

Shop assistants don't look at you when you're overweight. The other day I walked into one of those very high-end stores. There were racks of Colette Dinigans and Sass & Bide. Dresses that were so fragile they looked like they were made from cotton candy by a tafe student. The price tags were ridiculous, $2000 for a dress that looked like a frayed chamois. The anorexic girl at the counter had that hungry eyed stare of the skinny. Skinny people don't see fatties as individuals. We are all gross to them. She looked like a preying mantis, her giant lollypop head wobbling from side to side. She didn't look me in the eye at first and when she finally did it had that condescending, 'looking for Rockmans?' sneer. I think, *fuck her. Fuck her and the celery stick she's shoved up her arse.* So I grabbed a dress. A tiny one. A Colette Dinnigan. I took it to the change room.

Skinny bitch's head nearly wobbled off its post. She began pleading, 'No, no, no.' But I was already in the change room. You can hear me. There's nothing more satisfying than the sound of fabric struggling over fat rolls. The shop's techno mix was punctuated with high-pitched ripping as the Dinnigan lost the battle with my arse. I came out of the change room, one tit hanging out and both bum cheeks exposed. I am middle-aged Sophie Dahl before she got skinny. The shop assistant started to have a panic attack and gasped, 'Can I help you?' *Really. Now you want to help?* I smile innocently, 'Thank you, I don't think this is my size … do you have it in a six?'

The shop assistant seemed to be in a coma. There were actual bits of foam on the sides of her mouth. I know it's evil, but I do this once a month. I call it my feminist duty. It ensures that chubsters like me get good service. Or else they take out the store.

But no fatty wants to stay fat. I want to be thin and gorgeous and compassionless again. I want to be hotter than Magda. I want to wear my daughter's shorts. And I will. Right after I eat this cake.

# Secrets and lice

I've got a secret. I've got head lice. I've had them off and on for the past ten years. Not because I'm a crack whore or crazy cat lady, but because I have five kids. At our house we not only just scratch by financially each week, we literally scratch. Every Thursday I perch on the edge of the bathtub to perform the weekly nit harvest to determine who the mystery louse host is this week. Which child's head has these blood-filled parasites supped on? We like to make it competitive and run a bit of a lottery (or a nittery), where the kid with the biggest crop wins. I love it. There's something immensely satisfying about combing through your child's hair with one of those sharp metal claws they sell as nit combs and counting just how many bodies you wipe on the tissue. I'm like a serial killer. Ten adults, 16 juveniles and about 30 infants. I crush their bodies with my fingernails, feeling a tiny thrill every time I hear their abdomens pop. Then I flush them down the toilet. It's such a tidy way to dispose of a corpse.

I don't use chemicals. Not anymore. Besides it being a bit of a no-no amongst the felt-shoe wearing, organic mum squad, it's bloody expensive. After spending the equivalent of a family trip to Europe or a much needed face lift on hair lotions, mousses, electric nit zapping devices, nit repelling sprays, nit repelling affirmations (I am not a lice person, I deserve animal free hair), I realised that it's pointless. They always come back. Nothing stops head lice. The bald head gives 100 per cent protection from infestation but that's only until the hair grows back. Sure, it's nice to be nit free, but to be hair free as well is a bit extreme. You may no longer have head lice but the door has opened to a whole new raft of social problems. You become the poor shaved-head kid. 'Hey look, it's the Dalai Lama!'

If the stigma of being lice-ridden wasn't enough, try shaving off your kid's hair. If you're considering this as a more aggressive chemical-free approach I suggest you go the whole hog and get them to wear a T-shirt emblazoned with 'UNCLEAN'. It takes away that horrible anxiety you get worrying about if your kid is being bullied. This way you know they will be. It's a given.

No child has ever died from head lice. Shocking isn't it? No kid has ever lapsed into unconsciousness, or what could be called 'A Nit Coma' due to lice infestation.

the ultimate
mothering
evolution...
lice
combs for
fingers

'What happened to your sister?'

'Well, they drank all her blood and became like super lice and then they ate through to her brain.'

Lice are benign. Apart from being stupid itchy. That's about it. While children haven't actually died, there are some that have claimed to die from the embarrassment of actually having them. My stepdaughter Rachel, who has beautiful, long, thick brown hair, had lived a nit-free life until she joined my louse-ridden brood. So it was only a matter of time before my son Charlie's head lightly touched hers on the couch, thus building a tiny hairy bridge where lice could roam freely from skull to skull. Head lice which had spent the last five years on the overcrowded planet Charlie suddenly touched down on planet Rachel. A vast dark untouched wilderness. This was the place where nitties could start their master race!

At the slightest mention of lice Rachel was in tears. I'd never seen such a response. Perhaps she thought she wasn't worthy? I assured her that it wasn't something to be ashamed of. Like Zoe, Sophia and Charlie, she too was a 'chosen one'. I reassured her with my Buddha-like gaze and our family mantra: 'Don't worry little one, they will show the way.'

Rachel's mother sent emails complaining of what she refers to as 'the worst infestation' of lice she has ever seen. It's not explicit but the implication is that we are a bunch of dirty hippies who neglect their kids. And she is right. I'm far too busy packing a bong to pack lunches! Okay, I am being facetious, but social judgement around head lice makes me burn.

There is still so much shame associated with head lice. I reckon it's social conditioning to prepare us for the adult embarrassment of sexual diseases. I once had pubic crabs, an experience that left me feeling like my vagina was the landscape for some weird micro-sized H G Wells science fiction novel where the world was over run by twat-dwelling crustaceans. It was mortifying. I had to call in the pest man. (Although I think it was the same pest of a man who gave them to me in the first place!)

Now I see the crab has his place. Although I'm quite concerned that the popularity of the Brazilian may have rendered the humble pubic crab to the endangered species list. There's a perception, particularly by the childless and older members of the community that kids with head lice are dirty. That's simply not true. They're not dirty at all. Their mothers are.

No I don't change the kids' sheets, or air the pillows or wash hats. I'm far too lazy. Nor do I do what our chemical loving mother's did and up-end half a litre of kerosene on their poor beans. At our house we live with our lice. Sure, we occasionally reduce the numbers, but we have surrendered to the fact that we have lice. We love lice. We are lice.

They're not just lice, they're much more than that. We think of our louse less as parasites and more as pets. They are part of the family. And why not? Each of their microscopic bodies contains the exact same DNA as my children. Why are parasites so maligned? Surely feeding off the life force of another is what being a child is all about. I've breastfed all my babies, which technically means that kids are born parasites.

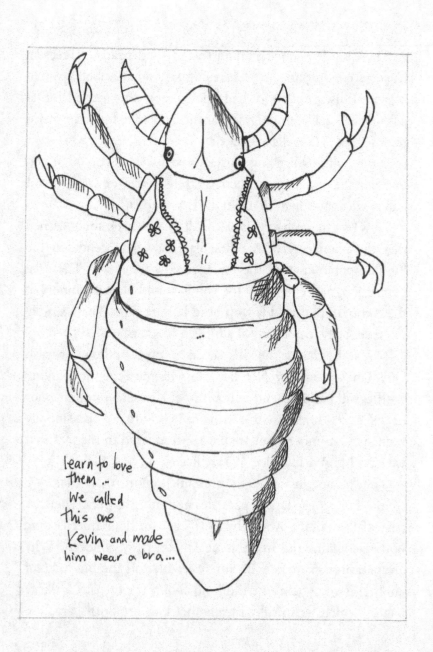

learn to love
them...
We called
this one
Kevin and made
him wear a bra...

I have teenagers who monopolise the lounge room with their crap TV, demanding money for mobile phone recharges so they can continue sending a trillion pointless texts to their equally pointless friends and insist I dedicate my weekends to the role of private chauffeur. I live with five healthy and very aggressive parasites and I haven't doused them in kero or tea tree oil or tried to flush them down the toilet. Yet.

Just last week one of Sophia's friends came over. I could tell she was a nice girl from a good home. At a glance her head looked clean. She didn't sit there scratching like us. We, the monkey family, assembled in front of the telly, gently holding the head of the other having a bit of a pick. It's very bonding. A few days later I received a call from a rather concerned mother.

'I'm sorry to have to call you, but I think you might have to check your children. After the weekend at your house Lilly was riddled with head lice.'

I've had this phone call a thousand times. 'Really? That's wonderful news. We thought there might have been something wrong with her. Congratulations, your daughter is the host of an entire ecosystem. She's been chosen ... Hello?'

# The agony, the ecstasy, crystal meth and you

What I would do if I were you:
Lie

Are you prepared to tell your children the truth? As parents we have this unrealistic expectation that our children will confide in us, sharing their darkest thoughts and confessing their most hideous misdemeanours. In theory, it cuts both ways. You have to be honest with your kids about your experiences. This policy of honesty works great guns if you spent your twenties living nil by mouth or twat. Meaning, if you were a boring, straight goody goody virgin then honesty is a road made for you. For the rest of us debauched piggies, fessing up opens the door for our kids to get away with myriad crimes. For example: 'Geez Mum, how can you tell me not to smoke pot when you had your first joint at 16?'

I have been honest with my kids about everything except drugs. Sex is easy. I was a slut. I lost my virginity to a school boy with a shock of blonde hair and a silver tooth at 15. It was awful, and so was he. After my initial heartbreak I realised sex was not only an act of love between two people, it could also be an act of war, where the invader was only interested in claiming new territory. I was always a troublemaker, and so developed a rather voracious sexual appetite fuelled by the thrill of the conquest and feelings of power. Particularly when it came to authority figures. At just 17 I'd bedded one school teacher, a Buddhist monk and a Catholic priest. The priest later turned out to be gay, and the Buddhist monk had a wife, which didn't do a lot for my self-esteem, or my belief in God. I've been pretty much agnostic ever since. I'm no longer interested in being a dominatrix; I prefer sexual congress to be non-denominational.

I was a studious kid. I was clever. I achieved. I was sporty. Up until that point I thrived on the approval and praise of my elders. It wasn't until my first year of university that I discovered my personal deficiency: I had no edge. So I grew my armpit hair, became a feminist and occasionally had sex with girls when an effeminate boy wasn't available. I also found drugs.

At first I was terrified. My own mother had no experience or knowledge of drugs; all her information came from films like *Reefer Madness* and *The Rose*. My adolescent drug education was based on the Nancy Reagan mantra: 'Just say no.' Otherwise you die. Just one puff and you could become an addict and life as you knew it was over. (Which was kind of true.)

At university I met people who smoked pot and dropped acid and they were all still alive. Not only that, they were studying law and medicine or psychology. They advocated the use of drugs as 'mind-opening' substances. Kind of like a door in the floor of your conscious mind.

I remember the first toke I ever had on a joint. I thought I was going to die. A hot rush of thick smoke filled my lungs and I opened that door in the floor and fell through. To the outside world I was the moron having such an intense laughing fit she fell off the couch. But in my internal world I'd gone through the looking glass and had emerged back via the rabbit hole. The world wasn't a linear narrative made up of black and white, right and wrong, yes and no. It was an infinite vortex of pink fluff where everything happened at exactly the same time.

My late teens and early twenties were the heyday of my drug taking years. Anything that could be imbibed was. I became such an unconventional thinker I could no longer tie my shoes. Instead I removed the laces and lived a 'no strings attached' lifestyle. (Except when I had to pay the rent. Then I'd ring my mother.) I had a great time. At the time I wasn't aware that in years to come I'd be a bloody role model. That I would be accountable for my behaviour, not to my mother, but to my bloody kids.

I'm not keen on my kids doing drugs. I know they probably will give it a go. But I don't really want to tell them about me. I don't want my happy times to normalise drug taking for my kids. Sure, I loved it. But it's risky. I could have ended up a drug-fucked acid casualty. After a decade living on 'the edge', I watched the clever friends retreat into family and career and grieved as the boundless ones fell into the abyss of mental illness, poverty, addiction and death. But the truth is, most of us survived. Most of us have kids. But that's not scary. That makes drugs sound downright pedestrian.

I don't regret my wayward past. Because in all honesty, I wasn't that wayward. I never ended up in jail. I never slept in the street. I never got arrested. I never overdosed. I never freaked out and tried to kill anyone.

I'd smoke pot and paint. When I was really stoned I'd clean. In fact I loved cleaning when I was off my chops. I don't think you can really comprehend the joy of a clean toilet cistern until you've spent two hours scrubbing the s-bend with a toothbrush. (The trick is to use your husband's toothbrush.)

I'd take ecstasy and dance. I snorted cocaine and talked about myself. I dropped acid and sat in the forest watching the trees melt. Hardly the stuff of TV anti-drug campaigns. In the end I didn't need to go to rehab, I just lost interest.

These days I'm a nice middle class mum with five kids, a mortgage and a dog. Nice mums generally don't admit that 20 years ago they were ecky heads. I happen to know a lot of mums who now wake up to pack lunches but used to wake up and pack bongs. Me included. In fact, the best joint I ever had was after pushing out my firstborn. I remember Rhett passed me a huge reefer, I had a toke and marvelled, 'Wow, I can make people!'

But relax, you don't need to ring DOCS. I'm not a crack whore. I'm a wheat-free, drug- and alcohol-free temple of judgement. I ride high on the healing horse of highly evolved consciousness. The closest thing I come to having a headrush these days is when I down two Diet Cokes and end up with heart palpitations. That wild, single, childless girl has gone forever.

In her place is the responsible, neurotic, over-protective and fearful mother. I never want my beautiful children to use drugs. I want their minds to stay tightly shut. Like Tupperware. Unlike my mother, my fear and drug education is based on experience. Drug taking was part of Generation X mainstream culture. The whole concept of my kids dabbling in the dark arts of consciousness unravelling leaves me sweaty.

What if the pot gives them psychosis and they end up with drug-induced schizophrenia? What if their eckies are cut with something nasty and they OD or dance to really bad music and can't tell? What if they become chronic coke users and turn into unbearable egotists? (If you've been to a chic inner city Sydney party then you'll know exactly what I'm talking about.)

Most of the drugs from my youth were around prying open the heart chakra. Ecstasy made us love people we despised and have sex with people we weren't attracted to. In my debauched youth, you were more likely to be harmed by an impromptu reflexology massage gone awry rather than an axe-wielding, ice-crazed psychopath.

As a parent ice scares me. I can't understand why you'd take drugs that make you angry and violent. You can get that sort of

picture of one of my finest moments as a responsible drinker...

action in any dysfunctional home for free. Where's the glamour in picking your scabs and burning yourself? I also don't get meth users, whose behaviour includes turning up at parties and beating people up, threatening emergency room workers and driving at 300 km per hour through a school zone. It just seems pointless. Whatever happened to the simple pleasures of, 'Wow, man I can hear colours!'

I am also extremely nervous about alcohol. Responsible drinking campaigns are hysterical. The only adults I've met who actually practise responsible drinking are sober alcoholics. They were responsible enough to stop.

Alcohol is all about being irresponsible. You don't have a few drinks and say, 'Jolly good, let's tidy the house.' No, you have a few drinks and scream, 'Bugger it! Let's get pissed and burn the shithole down!'

I often lie in bed at night freaking out about drugs. Sure, it's hard work teaching your baby to sleep. And yes it's challenging to cope with tantrums. But it's small fry when it comes to negotiating sex and drugs and alcohol. As parents, we have no strategies. Just saying 'No' doesn't work. Neither does saying 'Yes'. I've noticed that a lot of parents opt for the big comfy couch of denial by pretending it's not happening and saying, 'I didn't know!' I used to think it was a cop out. But it's not – it's bloody brilliant.

I know of parents who've taken drugs with their teenagers, offering a sort of initiation with mum and dad. A freaky product endorsement from the folks. I suppose if you had to drop acid

with your mum you'd put it off for a few years. Watching your mother cartwheeling in the nude may just be the perfect anti-dote to permissiveness. But I think the whole getting out of it with your kids is just creepy and irresponsible. I don't want to be some desperate 40-year-old with dilated pupils hugging kids at the skate park. And what if they become dependent on you as their source? I'm already tired of the 'Mum, can you bring me a glass of water?' demands. I reckon I'd pop a fuse if I heard, 'Mum, could you roll us a joint and crack open the Mars Bars?'

The other technique some parents adopt is the 'you can get drunk or smoke pot but you need to do it at home under our supervision.' What was once a home is now a privately funded shooting gallery. In general, I'm not comfortable with groups of kids coming to my home to get shitfaced. Can't they just meditate or play Boggle?

I don't believe the message that taking drugs is risky is actually getting through to kids. They think of themselves as bulletproof. When a kid crosses a road without looking and nearly gets hit by a car, you might scream, 'Christ, you nearly got hit by a car!' And the kid will reply, 'But I didn't!' As far as most young people are concerned if it didn't happen, well then it didn't happen. They're not interested in 'almost'. I think it's time we came up with a comprehensive campaign that targets kids where it really hurts. Clearly bad breath, possible psychosis and death are not strong enough deterrents. I have it. It's a very simple slogan: ALL DRUGS MAKE YOU FAT.

# The Clown Spirit

What I would do if I were you:
*Get regular exorcise*

When there's something wrong with your child you'll do anything to make them better. That's how I ended up engaging the services of an exorcist. It might seem a bit extreme, but when it came to behaviour modification I saw it as a drug-free alternative to Ritalin. And it worked.

This is one of my strangest parenting experiences, and in writing this book I never considered sharing it for an instant. I was concerned that the reader would be left imagining me dancing naked under a full moon around my Hills hoist. But on reflection, after considering that this is a book about disclosing the challenges, the failures and the struggles of parenting and family life without the necessity of providing solutions, I feel

Every dilemna deserves a pamphlet...

"she's a nice kid but her head spins round"

**What you should know...**
about Spiritual Possession.
a parent's guide:

"10 minutes a day of excorcise should make a big difference"

"am I crazy... or is my child possessed by evil demons... oh, what a relief!!!"

... to demystifying the mystifying

compelled to tell you. You must, however, promise never to tell a soul what I am about to reveal, otherwise I'll be labelled as a nutbag.

Let me begin by telling you a little about my spiritual status. I do not have one. I am not spiritual. I am not religious. I don't meditate. I don't pray to gurus. In fact I don't think I really know what I believe. And there in lies the problem. When it comes to the mysteries of life, death and the universe I have to admit, I just don't know. There must be a wonderful assurance in having a definitive point of view. Being an atheist or a religious zealot seems one and the same: they both come with assigned belief systems that offer the holder of those beliefs the comfort of knowing exactly what they think. There is no grey area. You either believe in God or you don't.

I've never been that certain. So I leave that part of my brain untended and hope that I'm never put in situations where I have to truly call my belief system into play.

This was all going along swimmingly until Sophia started displaying very unusual behaviours when she was in Year One at a small Catholic school. As the middle child she has always been a handful, but while capable of being challenging, it was unlike her to be constantly seeking conflict with her teacher. She was on detention for every day for six months.

I dreaded what her teacher was going to tell me next about her aberrant activities. Any parent of a child with behaviour problems knows the shame of being drawn aside by a teacher who then goes on to prove, beyond a shadow of a doubt, that you have birthed a monster. I don't react well in these situations. I can feel my blood pressure rising and am overwhelmed by a desire to headbutt the well meaning and earnest harbinger of parental failure.

Every day the teacher told me a new horror story. 'Today she jumped in the bin.' 'She stood on her desk.' 'She ran around the classroom for ten minutes knocking over chairs.' And my favourite, 'I walked into the classroom and she was standing on a chair on my desk imitating me!' The poor man was only a nerve ending away from a complete collapse. Somehow, my six-year-old had brought his 30 years as a teacher undone. He confessed that he didn't know what to do, that none of the behaviour techniques he was using, including continual lunch-time detentions, were working and that she was a continual unstoppable disruption. I was then referred to the principal and the school counsellor who asked veiled questions that seemed to infer she was being abused.

'Now Mandy, these kind of changes are very unusual and are often an indicator of something that may have happened in the home. Has she been left with anyone different? An uncle, or …' I realised they were asking if I'd been sub-contracting my after-school care to paedophiles. I assured them that things at home were pretty much the same and, as far as her father and I were aware, nothing untoward had happened to her.

Sophia's behaviour continued to become more unsettling. On one particular occasion the teacher told me he'd walked into the classroom and discovered her watching the TV on static. She flicked it on and off and ignored his requests to stop what she was doing. *Great,* I thought, *not only does she have some sort of behaviour problem, now she's re-enacting dodgy 80's movies. Poltergeist* here we come.

The weird thing was that her behaviour at home wasn't any better or worse than usual. There was nothing about how she behaved at home that seemed to correlate with what was happening at school. Maybe she didn't have a behaviour problem at all; maybe she was just a pain in the arse. Maybe she hated her teacher. After our daily run in's, I was getting close to hating him as well.

When I asked her what exactly was going on, her response was always the same. 'I can't help it, the Clown Spirit makes me do it. It's bigger than me.' I didn't really take any notice and guessed it was just another example of what a weirdo she was becoming. I took her to the doctor hoping she had ADD. Of course she didn't. I took her to a naturopath. A homeopath. Another doctor. Then a friend told me about some old bloke she'd taken her kids to, a chiropractor that did some sort of brain adjustments through spinal work. Or something like that. Once people start talking along these lines I tend to zone out.

But my friend had four, beautiful, well-adjusted children, with the eldest one already at university. She was also a straight Catholic woman, not someone I'd suspect of reading her own tarot and using affirmations instead of immunisations. So I decided to give it a go.

The chiropractor was a very unusual man. He was probably 70, maybe more. His pants were pulled up so high I was surprised he hadn't cut himself a new ball. Five long hairs were oiled and slicked over his bald spot in that way old men do to cover their shiny shame. He had no interpersonal skills. He spoke to Sophia softly, but completely ignored me. I had no idea what she was making of him. I stayed in the room in case he was a paedophile. He certainly looked like one.

He did a few adjustments on Sophia's spine, twisted a few nobs on some strange little metal box he had and then muttered, 'She has scoliosis. I've given her a back adjustment and I've closed the hole in her aura. She has a spiritual entity attached to her.'

That's a very strange statement to have to respond to. Do you say, 'Oh, I wondered what that was, I thought it was head lice, but turns out it's a poltergeist,' or 'Do they have entity removal kits at the chemist? Will I need a fine-toothed comb?'

I didn't know what to say, except, 'She did talk about a clown spirit but I thought she was joking. I just laughed.'

The chiropractor looked at me with an intense faded blue stare and shook his head. 'She was trying to tell you. You shouldn't have laughed.' I felt like dobbing myself into DOCS. 'Hello, it's Mandy Nolan, apparently my daughter is possessed and I ignored her cries for help. Lock me up in the cell next to Carrie's mum.'

I paid the $40 he asked for, waiting for the old charlatan to try and sell me a tincture or a pack of vitamins or request another visit. Instead all he said was, 'Just come back if it doesn't leave.'

Driving home in the car I felt nauseous. This was ridiculous. Some old cow cocky in a brown suit has told me my daughter has an entity attached. What a load of shit. But then I started to remember all the things she'd said to me the six months before, the throwaway statements that I'd dismissed as little girl nonsense.

'The Clown Spirit comes in through my side and then pushes itself out. I say "No, no," to it, but it makes itself bigger. It's bigger than me.' And when I'd roused on her and compared her to a kid who'd left school in kindergarten because she went a little nuts, Sophia said, 'That's because the Clown Spirit was in her and when she left it needed a home, so it went into me.'

Who do you tell this kind of stuff to? I felt like I was going mad. All I wanted was for my daughter to return to normal and all this crazy talk to stop. I wondered for an instant if I was in fact having a psychotic episode and projecting it onto my little girl. I rang my mother. She confirmed that I was nuts.

'It's just her way of verbalising her behaviour Mandy, she's a very clever little girl. She's externalising her lack of control over her behaviour.'

Mum doesn't believe in oogley boogley, although when I was eight years old and she was under the grip of born-again Christian types she once prayed over me to heal my earache. It worked. The pain shot out of my head and down her arm and it was gone. Mum and I never spoke about that incident again. It was so scary we both gave up ever believing in God.

clown spirit

It was all far too creepy. We existed much more happily as jaded cynics.

I told my then husband Russ. He's an atheist and just looked at me in disbelief. He gave a very accurate summation of the situation. 'Oh, for fuck's sake, Mandy.'

But no one told me what to do. They just passed judgement. Here was my child – only six, possibly possessed, possibly not. What do you do? It's not like there's a pamphlet down at the health centre which says, 'Do you think your child is possessed by an entity? Then complete this checklist:

* Does your child's head turn right round?
* Does your child have an aversion to crucifixes?
* Does your child react badly to sugar?

If you answered Yes to all of the above then your child is possessed.'

I was desperate for counsel. I went to the school principal and told her what I'd been told. The Catholics have a big history of exorcism, so I was curious about her response. Either she would accept what I was saying or she'd petition to have me committed.

Surprisingly, she was more open to the whole possession concept. 'Well, if we believe in God, and heaven and the afterlife, I suppose it's entirely possible,' she said.

Great. I don't believe in God. But I don't not believe in God. So what do I do?

I rang an exorcist. It's not like they're in the phone book, but I live in Byron Bay, so there's only two degrees of separation between you and a psychic healer. Raym was a friend of a friend. I'd teased him about his unusual occupation a decade or more before. He was rather pragmatic about it and didn't call himself an exorcist, but rather a 'spiritual healer'. When I rang him up and told him the story I was so embarrassed. I felt like an idiot. I kept waiting for Bruce Willis to pop out of the toilet and tell us we were already dead.

I didn't know what was going to happen next. Raym said, 'I don't need to see her but you have to ask the spirit if it will go to the light. If it says yes, then I can just do the clearing over the phone.' This was getting really frickin' weird. Then Ryam said 'Ask her now, and don't be frightened if her voice changes. You need to ask to speak to the Clown Spirit.'

I'd reached a point of desperation where I no longer cared that I didn't believe in spiritual possession. Or exorcists. Or demons. *You know what,* I thought, *I'll just do what works and bugger my belief system. I'll just give it a crack.*

I went to Sophia, who was in bed. I knelt down beside her and asked, 'Can I speak with the Clown Spirit?'

'Yes,' she says in this funny, little high pitched singsong voice. I was so scared I was shaking and I had tears running down my cheeks.

'Will the Clown Spirit go to the light?'

'Yes,' she replies again. I didn't ask anything else. I was not up for a conversation. I just wanted a nice clean eviction so I could go back to our normal life. I went back to the phone and told Raym.

'Great,' he said. 'Consider it done,' and hangs up.

From the very next day Sophia's behaviour returned to what our family considers normal and she never ever mentioned the Clown Spirit again. And as for me, I still can't fathom what the hell happened; except that it was so far out of my comfort zone it makes me shudder. But I'm still a sceptic. I'm not that easy to convince. I still don't believe in ghosts or God or spiritual healings, it's all far too out there for me. It takes more than a Clown Spirit to turn me into a cheesecloth-wearing, crystal-bowl ringing spiritualist.

This is just my story of something that happened to me that I still don't understand. I figured if someone should say something, it might as well be me. Because at the very worst you'll think it's a joke. I've done my research and nowhere in any parent books is there a single story about children with spiritual entities attached. Oh yes, there's toddler taming, conflict resolution with teens, how to do the sex talk, but when it comes to a good old-fashioned exorcism, the page is blank.

And who knows what actually happened? I suspect my mother was right: the whole thing was my daughter's rather precocious way of verbalising aberrant behaviour and that the sudden burst of attention was all she needed to get her little boat back on course. Or she was possessed by an evil clown. Doesn't really matter now. It was one of my greatest lessons in parenting. Sometimes you have to ditch your personal belief systems and go with what works. Even if it makes you look nuts.

Happy Exorcising.

# Just say no

Why are we frightened of saying no to our kids? When I was a kid, 'No' was the parental default setting. You barely needed to ask for anything because you knew that everything your heart desired was off limits. I grew up, as did the rest of my generation and the generations that preceded them, fully aware that I wasn't able to get what I wanted by conventional means. It called for covert operations. We connived clever plans to duck out early from school for a fag, or meet behind the bike shed for a quick genital fumble or lie about a Youth Group Meeting so we could sneak off to a party. The truth is though, I rarely did any of these things because the consequences of being caught far outweighed what small pleasures would be gained in the deception.

We are the generation of parents who believe we've established a relationship built on trust. It's not trust: it's spin. Kids are born strategists. And it's not their fault. It's unnatural for kids to be completely honest with their parents. Kids will tell us as much as they can get away with. They're the masters of PR and know how to do a good sell on any situation. Trust? That's what we tell ourselves we've built our relationships on … but really, isn't it more honest to say we haven't got a clue how to grow new people, and basically we're hoping that, rather than being totally responsible for the harvest, we've entered into a co-operative situation with the crop.

It's insane. We are the farmers of our own families, it's time we took responsibility for the seeds we've sown and tended our gardens with a little more care. We want to think our relationships are deeper and more meaningful than the ones we had with our parents because our kids have us by the short and curlies. We're scared of them. And now, after the Brazilian craze has swept the world, we don't even have a single short or curly left. We're fucked.

'Trust' is the slogan of soft-hearted parents who don't have the spine to say no. When they allow their adolescents what they call freedom and I call neglect, the usual catchphrase is, 'I allow them to go out at night to parties because I feel I can trust them.' Meanwhile their 14-year-old is sneaking a goon sack in their school bag and getting rat-arsed at lunchtime. Yeah. That trust thing is really working. If you live in denial about what is really happening in your world then trust is the ultimate panacea. You can believe that your kids are fine. Until they're not.

I see 'freedom' like a rope. If you let it out all at once your kid is at risk of falling of the first cliff and hanging themselves. Once you've let it out you can't turn around and pull it back in. You need to let it out in increments, and when they've shown some degree of competence and self-reliance, then they get a little more. Sure they'll make mistakes, but they're small ones that can be fixed – they're not dead on the roadside with three of their P-plater friends. But control freak parents beware: if the rope is too short they will choke to death.

Children by nature are born anarchists who'd rather be butt naked with their bum in the sun than suffer the confines of a nappy. It's the same with rules. My friend's daughter attends a Steiner school. She was bemused by the amount of attention the parental requests to allow their high school children the right to be shoeless received from the school staff. It appeared that some adolescents couldn't even manage to comply with a simple school policy of 'must wear shoes'. We're not talking ugly black leather foot containers; we're talking a shoe of their choice. Christ, if kids can't manage to comply with that, how will they ever manage to integrate in society? 'I'm not wiping my bum today because I don't feel I should have to.'

My kids think I'm strict, which is ridiculous. What they mean is that I set boundaries and there are limits on what they can do. 'I'm sorry, sweetheart, your friends can't smoke pot on

Setting firm boundaries is the cornerstone of effective parenting...

the lounge and I'd rather you didn't take photos of your breasts and post them on Facebook.' There are also consequences for behaviour. For example, Sophia is a born boundary rider. She hates rules. She can't believe they actually apply to her. Her school phoned me to tell me that she'd skipped class with another girl. I suspected they'd racked off to MacDonalds, which it turns out they did. And who wouldn't when it's just sitting there across the McRoad? So I waited for her to 'fess up but she says nothing all weekend. Then on Monday I ask her, 'Do you have something to tell me?'

'No.'

'Really? You really have nothing to tell me?'

Sophia looks at me stony faced, expressionless and disinterested. 'I said no.'

I nearly popped a gasket. 'Wrong answer!' I then revealed that I knew about her playing hookey at school and told her I was most upset that, given the opportunity, she didn't 'fess up. See, our relationship is built on Trust.

I gave one of those mother lectures that goes for about an hour. Then there's an intermission, popcorn, and then we're back in for the last session, which is basically a repeat of the first but usually not quite as emotional. Punishments are handed out. No sleepovers or playdates for a month. Sophia winces but she's okay. Then I add no Facebook for a month. She goes ballistic. She falls on the floor, kicking and screaming 'NOOOO!' Clearly this is a very, very effective punishment. Unplug the electrical umbilical cord that keeps them connected to the world wide web of parental deception and you have just regained your child!

I hate Facebook. Every night my kids tap into the cyber portal that allows every friend they've ever met into our home. It's so hard to parent when they're armed with an attitude they gleam from their peers. Every time they connect with their Facebook friends they disconnect from their family. Facebook is destroying family relationships. I'm going to destroy Facebook. Or at least learn to use it for parental purposes. I have my friends make themselves 'friends' of my children so that they can peruse their Facebook and alert me if something is amiss. And when Zoe was being really non compliant, I found the ultimate negotiation tool.

'Zoe, can you clean your room.'

Silence.

'If you don't clean your room now I am posting your home birth video on Facebook'. And so I did. You should have seen the comments: 'Love the furry hat'. In fact I was thrilled with the response, 63 people liked it!

So Sophia was banned from Facebook for a month. She was like an addict going through withdrawals. She lay on the floor in the foetal position. She couldn't get comfortable. She was restless. She was angry. This went on for a few days, but then she seemed to find a kind of inner equilibrium. She begins retreating into her room and spending time on her own. When I ask her what she is doing in there she says she is listening to her iPod. I hate them too but I couldn't rob her of every technological device. Although it

was tempting to replace it with something I would have had at her age and give her a taste of the good old cassette deck.

My intuition told me that things weren't completely right but I couldn't put my finger on it. Then one day Zoe was sitting on the lounge with her notebook when she got up to use the toilet, leaving her Facebook page open.

Charlie leans over and remarks, 'Hey Mum, I just looked at Zoe's Facebook here and it says what friends are online, and Sophia is.' That little shit, she's been using her iPod to go online! I had no idea the stupid thing had that capacity. You certainly couldn't do that with a cassette deck!

So I Facebook Sophia from Zoe's profile. 'Hi, s'up.' (See. I speak fluent teen.)

Sophia responds immediately, 'S'up w u?'

I feel like a cyber detective. 'This is Mummy, you are so sprung!' Then I walk into her room. There's a gap of maybe three seconds between the posting and my appearance in her doorway.

'You've been going on Facebook. I have proof. So what have you got to say for yourself?'

Sophia doesn't blink. 'It's Amber. I gave her my password.' My God, the girl is Richard Nixon re-incarnated. It's FacebookGate in my own home. That is the exactly the kind of situation that gives me such a huge dose of mental anguish it almost turns my brain inside out.

Everyone talks about the sleeplessness of having babies, the challenge of toddlers. I'd run a herd of 30 toddlers any day before I negotiated the mental badlands of parenting adolescents. This is mind-fuck territory. I've become a cop in my own home. I am never off duty. It's exhausting. That's what grandparents and aunts and uncles are supposed to be for, to fill the occasional shift so we can get some respite. But my extended family live too far away. It was my fault. I chose to have children away from my family. What a mistake. If I were to do it all over again I would never leave home. I'm 43 and I really need my mummy.

I used to be a bit of a wishy-washy type parent and the kids knew it. They knew if they sprung something on me at the very last minute I'd crumble because I couldn't bear disappointing them, and I wouldn't have time to do all the necessary parental phone verifications. I'd have to go with a nervous 'Yes', hoping that things didn't go pear-shaped. I don't do that anymore. I've got too many kids, and if you don't stand up for yourself and claim your adult status then it's like being pecked to death by ducks. You won't die straight away, but you'll be systematically worn down by years of constant badgering and emotional abuse.

If you want to know what's really happening, then start saying no. Be prepared for your kids to start to melt down. Furniture might be thrown. Expect insults about your weight, unkind feedback about your parenting skills and then, of course, the peer appraisal where you are informed that you are the only idiot parent who insists on calling other parents to check on teenage arrangements.

Saying no means you are going to have a shit weekend. If I just said yes and lied to myself that I could trust my daughter to make all the right choices even when she was in adult situations then I'd have a nice relaxing weekend. 'Sure, why don't you hitch to that party they're having in the forest, I'm sure you won't take ecstasy or drink alcohol. Stay away from the pot dealers and call Mummy if the knife-wielding ice freaks turn up. Have fun!' Instead I have said no to a party that everyone else is going to and consequently am having to duck hurtling objects on my way to the kitchen. The house is a war zone, and Mummy is battling the front line. Oh no, I'm down. I've just been hit by a hairbrush.

It's our job as parents to deliver our children to adulthood as intact as possible. Then they can make their own choices. It's certainly not an easy task, particularly when the major enemy in providing your child with the best start in life possible is, in fact, the child. Do you want your child to screw up their life by going out and getting drunk and then being raped and spending half their life in therapy unable to ever have successful relationships because they can't trust people and then developing a substance abuse issue to fill the hole and dying alone? There's only one answer to that question.

We as a community of parents really need to lift our game and take back some of the power in our family relationships. Maybe we need to remember we are not friends, we are parents. I'm not talking about ordering a brand new set of wooden spoons and beating the kids. I'm talking about being there for our kids and keeping them safe. One of my close friends is a youth worker, and she always asks her most at-risk kids what they want most. Without fail they say the same thing: 'boundaries and family'. So put that in your crack pipe and smoke it.

# Confessions of a mofo

Once upon a time kids spent a lot of time outside. Mothers kept their houses tidy by ensuring children were only permitted indoors when it was dark or rainy. From the minute the sun was up my brother and I were relegated to the backyard. It wasn't punishment. We didn't mind being outside because there wasn't actually anything to do inside. There were no iPods or computers or PlayStations. The sum total of our technological wizardry was a tape deck and a pop-up toaster. Sometimes for a thrill I'd pop a slice of wholemeal into the tape deck and ask my brother if he wanted to listen to Bread. Of course he was a baby at the time so he didn't actually get the joke.

We had a black and white telly but it only picked up two stations: a fuzzy regionally broadcast commercial station and the ABC. There was nothing remotely worth watching until *Dr Who* came on at 6 p.m. And by that time it was almost dark so we were finally allowed indoors.

We didn't have Facebook; we had flesh-and-blood friends. These were actual people who lived in your street. Streetbook. The thing about streetbook is that you could never be too discriminatory about who you played with. You didn't really have the kind of options kids have today. If someone annoys one of my daughters, in one click they've been unfriended and as far as my daughter is concerned, they no longer exist. Not so in the real world. Very often you were forced to make friends with people you didn't like purely based on the fact that they lived next door. Proximity won over personality every time.

I used to have a lot of fun at the expense of a chubby little girl called Sonia. I remember inviting her over for afternoon tea. She was terrified of spiders so it presented me with the perfect opportunity to introduce her to the new set of rubber arachnids I'd acquired in my latest Easter show bag. I arranged them in various stages of attack on the clock which sat bang centre of our 1970s laminex buffet.

Just as Sonia was about to bite into a cupcake I casually asked her the time. Like I had a bus to catch or something, even though I was only six. Sonia turned toward the clock. It took her about ten seconds to register that the clock was alive with spiders. She started screaming and ran out of the house sobbing.

I decided that seeing as she couldn't fulfil our arrangement, it was only fair that I ate her cake. I was always mean to poor Sonia. I'm proud to say I didn't lie in my bedroom writing nasty things on her home page; if I wanted to be nasty to Sonia I'd jump the fence and go directly to her home.

My kids are scared of the backyard. Whenever I suggest that they go outside and kick the ball or maybe even sit in the sun they look at me with disbelief. 'But there are snakes out there.'

Of course there are snakes out there. That's the point. It's interesting. It's the outside. I try to be encouraging. 'If you're scared of snakes just bang on the steps and you'll frighten them off.' I don't think that was the encouragement they were after.

When I had kids I imagined myself in the backyard with them. I'd be tending a vegetable patch and they'd be jumping on the trampoline or building a hideout under the picnic table. I imagined we'd be these healthy, outdoorsy types who played badminton and volleyball. My girls would be picking flowers and my son would be playing cars in the dirt. In reality I seem to spend most of my life at the clothesline and they're on the couch watching TV.

Thanks to the real estate boom and the sudden hike in the average Australian house block, the backyard is becoming a thing of the past. Instead of a quarter-acre block where you could swing a cricket bat or have a game of footy, most suburban families are relegated to enjoying the delights of a foot massage from their 2-metre square Zen rock garden and fun under the hose is replaced by jamming aforementioned rocks into the

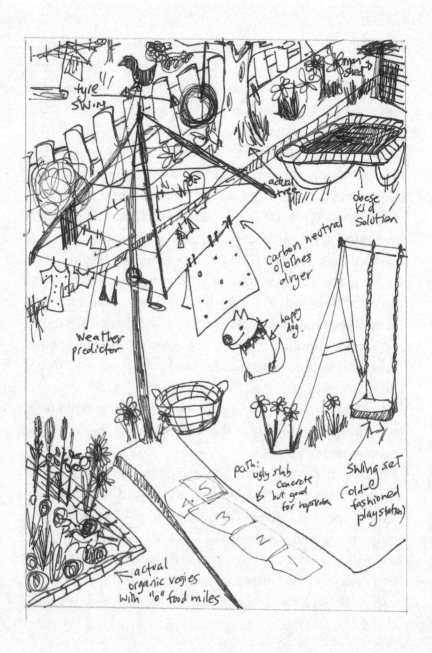

authentic 'made in China but bought from Bunnings' Buddha water feature.

When I was a kid, backyards had trees where you could build cubbies, and there was a vegetable patch that produced actual food, real organic food that you grew yourself. You didn't even realise it was organic. That's how organic it was. There was always a giant mound of grass clippings that your mum or dad would set fire to every month in a backyard bonfire. I loved the monthly fires. I lived in the bush so there was always the risk that someone's burn-off would get out of control, particularly as it turned the average law-abiding family into instant arsonists: 'Let's burn the old couch'; 'What about the stereo?'; 'Or Nanna?'

When I was a kid, backyards weren't attractive. (Neither were kids. Is it Photoshop or have people just got a whole lot better looking in the last 20 years?) But backyards, like kids, didn't need to look good, they were at the back. (Or outside.) No-one could see them. If you wanted to impress people you tarted up your front yard. A swan fashioned from an old tyre or a letterbox hanging on a stiff chain generally did the trick. Backyards were purely functional: they had a Hills Hoist, a shed, maybe a set of swings, the corpse of a dismembered vehicle and a selection of makeshift crucifixes denoting the whereabouts of deceased pets. There is no place for this kind of unattractive chaos in our new *House and Garden* lifestyles. Backyards are not about being outside, they are about 'outdoor living'. Stylists decry: 'We make the outside like the inside.' It means we make it sanitised and safe

and pretty. Somewhere attractive to grow our new generation of obese, backyard-deprived offspring. Outdoor living. What a wank. Ask a homeless person about their experience of outdoor living and I think you'll get a very different response to the average *Better Homes & Garden* reader.

Outdoor living is not about having somewhere for your kids to play, it's about having people over for a chardonnay while enjoying the ambience only a water feature can bring. What is this obsession with water features? For women who've given birth to four children there is nothing relaxing about a bloody water feature. It's an urgent reminder that I need to do a whole lot more work on my pelvic floor. The constant uncontrollable desire to urinate is not ambient. It's torture. Water torture.

Kids just don't fit in this new designer backyard fad. Kids are unsightly and unless you've managed to dress them in white T-shirts and denim (like photographers insist in those ghastly family photos everyone seems to have), then you need to keep them in one of your IKEA child storage compartments.

I hate those reality backyard renovation TV shows where a family gets sent away and then a team comes in and completely wrecks a perfectly functional space. I mean they've got a giant labrador – where's Bessie gonna shit now you've paved paradise? I want to create my own version of a reality renovation show, except I'll take a more 1975 approach. I'll show up at a very nice housing estate and wait until a family goes away for the weekend. While they're gone I'll install a stinky fishpond, a burnt out car and a chook pen. Just wait for that big reveal!

The reality is that any normal family can't maintain a designer space. Six months on there's sheets hung out to dry on the new outdoor settings and someone's decapitated Buddha with a soccer ball.

I mean, wouldn't it be better if we all spent a lot more time in our backyards rather than 'on' them? Okay, what I'm really trying to say is I'm jealous. My backyard looks like crap.

# The mother woman

Being a mother still shocks me. The other day I caught sight of a woman in the street who had her tracksuit pants pulled up just a tad too high (I call that natural contraception … if you can get any action, then you bloody deserve it), two inches of grey-black regrowth at the base of her dyed blonde hair and wearing thongs. She was pushing a screaming kid in a pram, which was loaded in shopping. There was a bunch of kids trailing behind her. I thought *God, women let themselves go.* If she hadn't taken up so much space on the pavement, she'd be invisible. I mean, why would you keep having all those children? What man would come home to that she-devil and find her remotely attractive? Then I realised that it was not just some woman at all. It was me. I was passing unkind judgement on my reflection in the shop window – *I* was the mother. The internal picture of myself didn't match the reality.

Facebook is a firsthand glimpse at people's internal pictures. Have a look at the profile pics that people choose to use. They are usually at least 10 years younger than the person, or were taken at an angle that makes them look 20 kilos lighter. According to Facebook, we are all a heck of a lot better looking than we actually are. Basically, Facebook is a bunch of people living in the past, pretending they're still hip. I know. I'm on Facebook. In my profile pic I look fabulous. I'd never post a pic of what I look like right now. I know what the posts would be: 'Don't be offended, but you've been unfriended!'

Mums aren't just one big anomalous group. We've diversified according to our own personal mores. This has resulted in the creation of our own particular mumsy subcultures. While the job description is still fairly much the same, it would seem that the essential criteria has broadened. It's not the fifties anymore. Mums don't wear starched aprons, bake biscuits and live a secret double life as S&M leather whores. Mothering is no longer just a duty; it's a lifestyle choice. How you choose to do it is really up to you. When people ask about what sort of mother you are, they don't want to know if you are over-protective or a boundary setter. What they are really asking is if you are a self-focused yummy mummy, a heartless career bitch or a flappy armed canteen controller?

## The Yummy Mummy

These women are awful. I know. I used to be one. I still want to be one. After my first daughter Zoe was born I was pencil thin. I wore micro minis with platform shoes and tight T-shirts. I was a mother who didn't want to look like a mother. I remember the spiteful eyes of other older mums as I bent to pick up my toddler and revealed a well-tanned ass in a flimsy g-string. If I did the same thing now I'd take out half a suburb. Used to be I'd bend over to pick up 5 cents. These days, I won't bend for anything less than $2. And if you do catch sight of my knickers, they're more likely to be misshapen beige control tops than a lacy thong. They are Victoria's Real Secret.

Yummy Mummies are perfect. With their impossibly flat post-baby tummies, their fake tans and their whitened teeth, being beautiful is their number one priority. These are the mums you see running at breakneck speed with their jogging prams, their two-week-old infants at risk of shaken baby syndrome. These are the mums who don't work because in between going to the gym, looking after a new baby and getting weekly Brazilians, there's just no time! These are the women you see in cafés, meeting with groups of other Yummy Mummies and their equally annoying baby chino-supping children. It's funny to watch because it seems as though none of them actually like each other. They're only truly happy when one of their Yummy Mummy friends gets fat.

The kids of Yummy Mummies have groovy haircuts. The baby boys wear tight singlets and leather necklaces and baby girls are in Country Road. They have pretentious names like Cash or Wolfgang or Montana. I often wonder if naming the baby was less about thoughtfully creating a moniker a person carries for life and more about branding an important accessory. A kid with a cool name makes you cool. Yummy Mummies tend to have young children. The older they get and the more children they have, basically the less yummy they become. And that's when the daddies leave to find new Yummies. The Yummies eventually devolve into one of the other Mummy types.

## The Fat Tummy Mummy

These are the mums who've let themselves go. There are no trips to the gym. Fat Tummy Mummies go to the supermarket. They no longer shop for the latest skinny jeans or fight for Prada handbags on eBay. They buy furniture. They dream about homewares. The Fat Tummy Mummy has assumed the maternal shape of a Babushka, the waistline a distant memory and diabetes just a slice of white bread away. Fat Tummy Mummies are selfless. They have made mothering a career and channelled all their brilliance and management skills into their family. They are soft-shelled, hard-headed matriarchs. You find them waiting in their cars outside ballet classes, football practice or guitar lessons, writing meal plans on their iPhones. They've replaced mico-managing their bodies with micro-managing their homes. They are dedicated to their children.

They never miss parent–teacher meetings. Their children are well-adjusted high achievers. (Even the ones who grow up to be junkies.) All their meals are prepared from a *Donna Hay* book. And at night, when they get in bed, they wear a big cotton nightie and cuddle up to a water bottle for their sciatica. Their husband sleeps on the couch.

## The Dummy Mummy

These are the stupid mums. The ones who won't immunise their kids for whooping cough, but insist on taking their hacking child to the local park. These mums won't let their babies eat or wear chemicals, but they're still smoking pot. And breastfeeding. These mums let their four-year-old daughters play games with the family labrador while it's eating. These mums won't put up a pool fence because it wrecks the feng shui and won't send their kids to schools that believe children shouldn't use black crayons. (Pretty tough if you're a black kid trying to paint a self portrait.) These are the mums who take ecstasy with their teenagers so they can experience drugs 'together'. These are the mums who let their 12-year-olds go to parties where there's alcohol. These are the mums who believe that the texts from an ex-girlfriend on their husbands' phone are just wrong numbers.

## The Slummy Mummy

These mummies just can't cope. They're drowning in housework. The bins are spilling onto the floor, the dishes are mounted up on the sink, on benchtops and in boxes on the kitchen table. The sheets haven't been changed. Ever. There's dog poo on the carpet and a stinking bin of nappies at the door. The washing made it off the line, but remains in huge piles on the couch. It looks like a Vinnie's sorting room. Slummy Mummy finds a space and drinks her tea. Somehow her child manages to survive the incidences of near choking on the broken debris that litters the floor and in the process develops a rock solid immune system.

## The Bummy Mummy

Meet the borrowers. At any time of day or night there's a knock at the door and one or all of the following questions might be asked:

'Would you have a cup of sugar?' 'A bandaid?' 'Paw Paw ointment?'

'Do you have any potatoes? We're making a salad and the shop's shut?'

'Do you have any pads? Siana's got her period.'

'Do you have a spare bottle of red?'

'Do you have anything I could wear?'

'Can I borrow the hair iron?'

'Are you using your car this weekend?'

'Can you mind the kids tonight, I've got a headache?'

Some mummies hate asking for help but not the Bummy Mummy. Bummies ask for what they need. Constantly. Only problem is, real bummies don't return the borrowed item, or the favour.

## The Plummy Mummy

These are the posh mummies. The rich girls. The mummies who went to good schools and got a proper education. (Or poor girls who were smart enough to marry well.) They wear designer clothes, but they're understated. Their furnishings are minimalist. Their crockery matches their platters and their platters match their teeth. All perfectly white, like their towels. Their sheets are Egyptian cotton. Their vegetables are organic and bought in a wicker basket at the local farmer's market. They read Deepak Chopra. They attend yoga classes and meditation retreats. They're involved in charity work. They host fabulous dinner parties and occasionally go in for a partner swap. Their kids speak a second language. They're incredibly busy doing very little. I love them. They're super intelligent and super fragile and super disappointed with their lives all at the same time. I have always coveted the life of plummy mummies. It was never destined to be my lot.

## The Chummy Mummy

This is the mum pack you just won't break. You are either on the inside of the Chummy Mummies or the outside. I've always been on the outside. Chummy Mummies congregate at school pick-up time talking about their kids, they make playdates that your children are not invited to, they go out with the 'girls' for drinks and they are all members of the same book club. Chummy Mummies car pool. They pick up each other's kids. They know all the teachers on a first name basis. They are usually pretty sporty. Or at least their kids are, so they're often the coaches and run the canteens, the fundraisers and the weekly meets. Chummy Mummies are very friendly. But they're practical. They only have room for so many mummy friends. I've always sworn far too much to be invited into the inner sanctum of the Chummies.

Sometimes, though, I make special guest appearances because I'm a bit of a novelty. 'Wow, did you know Mandy has a new partner? How many dads is that now? Three! My goodness. How do you manage?' I generally down another glass of chardonnay and gush, 'I'm only just warming up – where's your husband?' The door closes and I don't get another invitation for a decade.

## The Gummy Mummy

These mummies are the toothless tigers. When their kid picks up a cricket bat and whacks another kid on the head they coo sweetly, 'Jackson, Mummy says no!' Gummy Mummies never yell. They don't threaten. They don't ground. They beg softly. When their cervix dilated 10 centimetres to release their genetic progeny, the tidal wave of unconditional love completely annihilated the rage room in their control centre. Fiercely overprotective if someone else jumps in and chastises their little angel, gummies are just in complete awe of their precious little monsters.

# The not Very Calmy Mummy

Have you ever wondered what it's like to live in a constant state of low-level anxiety? Meet a Not Very Calmy Mummy. These women panic about everything. As far as they're concerned, they are the only barrier between the world, their child and certain death. They catastrophise the common cold into a midnight emergency room visit to check for meningococcal. If a head is bumped they're examining the iris with a torch for dilation diagnosis. A mosquito bite is only one scratch away from blood poisoning. They fear the sun, snakes, swimming pools, processed foods, M-rated movies, unnatural fibres, bicycles, sugar, paedophiles and peanuts. Their kids don't have sleepovers. They can't. They're breastfed until high school.

# The March to my Drummy Mummy

These Mummies scare me. They are insane, power-wielding control freaks. Their children have been moulded into muppets requiring parental operation. Their children are a second shot at the life they never got. These mummies are clever. They know that the best way to manipulate is not through anger and threats but emotional torture. Compliance through crying. Even their meals are garnished with guilt.

# The Tsunami Mummy

Call DOCS, there's a Tsunami Mummy in aisle three! This is parenting as a natural disaster. These women clearly don't enjoy parenting, or they think that yelling at their kid is a spectator sport. Do they bring their children into the public arena purely to abuse them? Do they think we're all silently cheering, 'Top work! You give it to him, love!' I've watched these women wheeling their screaming two-year-olds around K-Mart screeching, 'Shut up you little shit or I'll slap ya,' and I've thought, *How about we close the book on this one and just slap you right now, you stupid cow.* If I worked in child protection, I'd hang around shopping malls and supermarkets. You'd catch one every ten minutes.

## The Crummy Mummy

These mums are shit. They're the ones who drop their kids off for a playdate and then arrive five hours late for pick up with the feeble excuse of, 'I got pissed and had to wait to sober up before I could drive.' Crummy Mummies don't read school newsletters. They never turn up at assembly when their kids get an award. They forget to photograph their kid's first day of school. They make boring lunches. Sometimes they don't even put in a water bottle, and if they do they use one of those toxic jobs made of Chinese plastic. Crummy Mummies don't always make their kids wear seatbelts. Or bike helmets. Crummy Mummies give their kids chocolate bars in the supermarket to stop them screaming. When they don't stop screaming, Crummy Mummies leave them there and go home. Crummy Mummies don't wash school uniforms and have to use a kitchen sponge to remove stains. Crummy Mummies hate dance recitals and spend the whole time complaining about how boring it is watching a bunch of kids trussed up like Jean Michelle-Benet prance around in tutus. Crummy Mummies serve baked beans on toast for dinner. Twice a week. Crummy Mummies send their vomiting children to day care so they don't have to cancel their pedicure. Crummy Mummies resent housework. They borrow pocket money from their kids' piggy bank to buy weed and smoke it in front of their kids. Crummy Mummies watch *Wolf Creek* with their ten-year old and let them sleep on the couch. Crummy Mummies avoid parent-teacher meetings, they never do canteen and when other kids come for sleepovers they let them stay up all night. Crummy Mummies complain that their kids aren't gifted, that they don't win races at swimming carnivals or public speaking competitions. Crummy Mummies tell their teenage dautghters they're getting fat to cut back on lunch money and some Crummy Mummies even have affairs with other people's daddies.

It's hard to be brutally honest and admit just what sort of Mummy you are. I'm an ex-Yummy who looks like a Fat Tummy but is actually a Crummy. I also have moments as a Dummy, a Gummy and a Not Very Calmy.

As a mother it's so hard to admit your failings. When I had my first child I remember thinking that there was no way I was going to screw this up like other people do. I was going to be perfect. I was going to be the best mother ever. My child would grow up well balanced and nurtured and talented. She would want for nothing. As it turned out, by the age of two she'd been subjected to her parents continual fighting and her father's heroin addiction.

It took me some time to realise that the challenges my children face, their struggles and their flaws, are part of what makes them human. And yes, to some degree it has been my decisions, my choices, my weaknesses and lack of boundaries, that have fed them. I love all my children beyond belief. But I make mistakes. I yell. I blame. I threaten. I curse. I cry. I complain. I throw tantrums. I sulk. I bitch. I lie. And if I was to tell the complete and utter truth about my experience of being a mother, I'd have to admit that I haven't got a clue what I'm doing. Basically I'm making it up.

I'm just getting better at it.